my revision notes

Renewals 0
Y LIBRARIE
TURNED ON
ARK

Cambridge National Level 1/2

CHILD DEVELOPMENT

Miranda Walker

HODDER

Haringey Libraries	
NN	
Askews & Holts	18-Mar-2019
305.231	
	3400027082

...ng for permission to reproduce copyright material.

© ShutterDivision/stock.adobe.com; Fig. 2.2 © MBI/ Alamy Stock Photo; Fig. 2.3 © kzenon – 123RF; Fig. 2.4 © auremar/stock.adobe.com; Fig. 2.10 © Rafael Ben-Ari/123RF; Fig. 3.2 © Tomorrow's Child UK Ltd; Fig. 3.3 © ka-chan/stock.adobe.com; Fig. 3.5 © Jules Selmes/Hodder Education; Fig. 3.6 © JenkoAtaman/stock.adobe.com; Fig. 3.7 © Andrew Callaghan/Hodder Education; Table 4.1 © Public Health England, 2017, licensed under the Open Government Licence 3.0; Fig. 4.1 © IAN HOOTON/SCIENCE PHOTO LIBRARY/GETTY IMAGES; Fig. 4.2 © soupstock/stock.adobe.com; Fig. 4.3 © all_about_people/Shutterstock; Fig. 4.4 © Jules Selmes/Hodder Education; Fig. 4.6 © Jules Selmes/Hodder Education; Fig. 4.7 © spotmatikphoto – Fotolia; Fig. 5.1 © Andrew Callaghan/Hodder Education; Fig. 5.2 British Standards Institute; Fig. 5.3 BHTA; Figure 5.4 © John Gustafsson – made by myself based on the specifications in EN 71-6:1994; Fig. 5.5 © European Commission; Fig. 5.8 © Jules Selmes/Hodder Education; Figs. 5.9, 5.10 © Andrew Callaghan/Hodder Education; Fig. 5.11 © Andy Dean – Fotolia.

Every effort has been made to trace all copyright holders, but if any have been inadvertently overlooked, the Publishers will be pleased to make the necessary arrangements at the first opportunity.

Although every effort has been made to ensure that website addresses are correct at time of going to press, Hodder Education cannot be held responsible for the content of any website mentioned in this book. It is sometimes possible to find a relocated web page by typing in the address of the home page for a website in the URL window of your browser.

Hachette UK's policy is to use papers that are natural, renewable and recyclable products and made from wood grown in sustainable forests. The logging and manufacturing processes are expected to conform to the environmental regulations of the country of origin.

Orders: please contact Bookpoint Ltd, 130 Park Drive, Milton Park, Abingdon, Oxon OX14 4SE. Telephone: (44) 01235 827720. Fax: (44) 01235 400401. Email education@bookpoint.co.uk Lines are open from 9 a.m. to 5 p.m., Monday to Saturday, with a 24-hour message answering service. You can also order through our website: www.hoddereducation.co.uk

ISBN: 978 1 5104 3469 1

© Miranda Walker 2018

First published in 2018 by

Hodder Education,

An Hachette UK Company

Carmelite House

50 Victoria Embankment

London EC4Y 0DZ

www.hoddereducation.co.uk

Impression number   10   9   8   7   6   5   4   3

Year   2022   2021   2020   2019   2018

All rights reserved. Apart from any use permitted under UK copyright law, no part of this publication may be reproduced or transmitted in any form or by any means, electronic or mechanical, including photocopying and recording, or held within any information storage and retrieval system, without permission in writing from the publisher or under licence from the Copyright Licensing Agency Limited. Further details of such licences (for reprographic reproduction) may be obtained from the Copyright Licensing Agency Limited, www.cla.co.uk

Cover photo © dpaint – stock.adobe.com

Typeset in India.

Printed in Spain.

A catalogue record for this title is available from the British Library.

Get the most from this book

Everyone has to decide his or her own revision strategy, but it is essential to review your work, learn it and test your understanding. These Revision Notes will help you to do that in a planned way, topic by topic. Use this book as the cornerstone of your revision and don't hesitate to write in it: personalise your notes and check your progress by ticking off each section as you revise.

Tick to track your progress

Use the revision planner on pages 4 and 5 to plan your revision, topic by topic. Tick each box when you have:

- revised and understood a topic
- tested yourself
- practised the exam questions and checked your answers.

You can also keep track of your revision by ticking off each topic heading in the book. You may find it helpful to add your own notes as you work through each topic.

My revision planner

R018 Health and well-being for child development

LO1: Understand reproduction and the roles and responsibilities of parenthood

		REVISED	TESTED	EXAM READY
1.1	The wide range of factors that affect the decision to have children	☐	☐	☐
1.2	Pre-conception health			
1.3	Roles and responsibilities of parenthood	☐	☐	☐
1.4	Recognise and evaluate methods of contraception, their efficiency and reliability			
1.5	The structure and function of male and female reproductive systems	☐	☐	☐

LO2: Understand antenatal care and preparation for birth

2.1	The roles of the different health professionals supporting the pregnant mother	☐	☐	☐

LO1: Understand reproduction and the roles and responsibilities of parenthood

1.1 The wide range of factors that affect the decision to have children

REVISED

Before deciding to have children, a couple will want to be sure that they understand and are ready for the roles and responsibilities that come with parenthood. To ensure they do not conceive before they are ready, and to know what to expect when they do try to conceive, couples need a good understanding of reproduction and contraception.

Features to help you succeed

Exam tips

Expert tips are given throughout the book to help you polish your exam technique in order to maximise your chances in the exam.

Common mistakes

The author identifies the typical mistakes candidates make and explains how you can avoid them.

Now test yourself

These short, knowledge-based questions provide the first step in testing your learning. Answers are provided at the back of the book.

Definitions and key words

Clear, concise definitions of essential key terms are provided where they first appear.

Revision activities

These activities will help you to understand each topic in an interactive way.

My revision planner

R018 Health and well-being for child development

REVISED   TESTED   EXAM READY

LO5: Know about child safety

REVISED   TESTED   EXAM
                     READY

Success in the examination

Sample practice questions and commentary

Glossary

Now test yourself answers

LO1: Understand reproduction and the roles and responsibilities of parenthood

1.1 The wide range of factors that affect the decision to have children

REVISED

Before deciding to have children, a couple will want to be sure that they understand and are ready for the roles and responsibilities that come with parenthood. To ensure they do not conceive before they are ready, and to know what to expect when they do try to conceive, couples need a good understanding of reproduction and contraception.

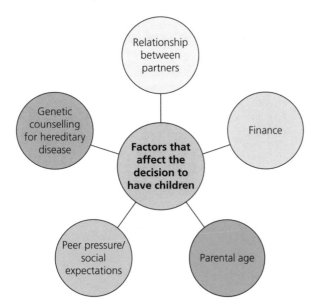

Figure 1.1 Factors that affect the decision to have children

The relationship between partners

The relationship between partners is a very important consideration. Couples deciding to start a family will generally have been together long enough to form a happy, stable, caring and secure relationship based on love and trust. The couple will share their lives and be committed to one another. They will also share respect, loyalty and priorities.

These things are important because:

- Parents should trust each other's ability to make the major life changes necessary to become a reliable and responsible parent.
- Parents should feel confident that they can cope with the demands of being a parent.
- Caring for a child can be exhausting, overwhelming and challenging at times.

- This is especially so when the baby is young and the parents are likely to be inexperienced and very tired.
- Couples will need to talk through any problems together.
- Couples will need to share their feelings honestly and respectfully.
- Couples will need to support one another in times of difficulty.

Partners need to think carefully about whether each wants to start a family because:

- All children need to feel wanted and loved.
- If one partner has a child for the sake of the relationship or to make their partner happy, they might feel resentful in the future.

Finance

Finance is an important factor when deciding to have children. Raising a child is very expensive.

- The most expensive years are between the ages of one and four, when parents spend an average of £63,224 on their child.
- Education is the most expensive aspect, including school uniforms, lunches, trips and equipment (private school fees will add more expense).
- Feeding children also costs a significant amount of money – around £19,004 from birth up to the age of 21 years.
- Research shows that the average costs of bringing up children are rising.
- Parents approach finances differently, but in most families one or both parents will work to earn the money needed to live.
- Part-time work can range from a few hours to several days each week.
- It is most common for the mother to work part-time and to care for the children part-time, but the number of stay-at-home fathers is on the rise.
- A registered childcare provider may provide childcare. Parents have to pay for this and it is expensive. The government funds 30 hours of childcare per week for three- and four-year-olds. Families in receipt of certain benefits are entitled to 15 hours of childcare per week for two-year-olds.

> **Exam tip**
>
> A question on finances may ask about the expense of childcare. Working parents are likely to spend around £70,466 on childcare and babysitting costs throughout a child's life. The most expensive childcare years are when the child is under two.

Parental age

Age of the mother

As a woman ages, her ability to conceive declines.

- The decline in her fertility is more rapid after the age of 35 years.
- After **menopause**, she will no longer be able to get pregnant.
- Some fertility experts have been warning women to start their families by the age of 30 to give themselves the best chance of getting pregnant.

Age of the father

A man's age has less of an effect on his ability to reproduce.

- Men produce sperm all their adult life.
- As long as they are physically capable of sexual intercourse, men can father children.

> **Menopause** – when a woman stops having a reproductive cycle.

Younger and older parents

Table 1.1 Comparing the experiences of younger and older parents

Younger parents	Older parents
• May be healthier and fitter, with more energy and a longer life expectancy. • May recover from pregnancy and birth faster (mother only). • Less likely to have a child with Down's syndrome. • May find it easier to return to studying/career after having a family. • May have family members such as parents who are younger themselves and more able to help out (e.g. with babysitting). • Less likely to be financially secure and to have a stable home. • May not yet feel ready for parental responsibilities. • May not yet be in a secure relationship. • May resent needing to give up a large part of their social life.	• More likely to be financially secure. • More likely to be mature, relaxed and confident about parenthood. • Have increased life experience, increasing their ability to handle challenges. • More likely to have established a career, completed training/qualifications before starting a family. • May recover from pregnancy and birth more slowly (mother only). • More likely to have a child with Down's syndrome (if the mother is over the age of 35). • More likely to have less energy.

Peer pressure/social expectations

Couples can feel pressured by peers to have a baby if:

- several members of a friendship group have babies, leaving them feeling excluded
- there is social expectation from friends and family for a couple to start a family
- people are surprised by a couple who do not want children.

What is right for the couple should always be the most important consideration.

Genetic counselling for hereditary diseases

Genetic disorders are inherited. They can include:

- Down's syndrome
- cystic fibrosis
- sickle cell anaemia
- muscular dystrophy.

Parents at risk of having a child with a genetic disorder will be offered genetic counselling (tests); for example:

- if parents already have a child who has a genetic disorder or congenital defect (heart defect)
- if there is family history of birth defects, genetic disorders or some forms of cancer
- if there have been repeated miscarriages or problems getting pregnant
- if there is a blood relationship between the partners (for example, cousins)
- if a parent's ethnic background is one in which genetic disorders are more likely.

> **Genetic disorders** – disorders inherited from one or both parents.

Exam tip

A question on genetic counselling may ask about how hereditary diseases are passed on. Some can only be passed on by the mother and some can only be passed on by the father. They are most commonly passed on through either the egg or the sperm.

Now test yourself

TESTED ☐

1. State **three** factors that affect the decision to have children.
2. Explain why finance is an important consideration for a couple deciding when to have a child.
3. Discuss the possible advantages of being an older parent.
4. Give **two** examples of when a couple will be offered genetic counselling.

1.2 Pre-conception health

Pre-conception health significantly impacts on the health of a baby, sometimes throughout its life. Addressing any health concerns before trying for a baby gives the child the healthiest start possible.

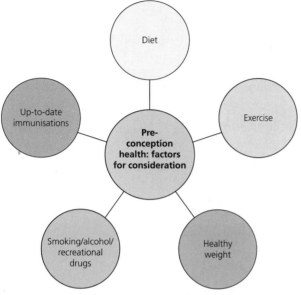

Figure 1.2 Factors for consideration relating to pre-conception health

Diet

A healthy diet is vital for the mother before and during pregnancy. The baby is reliant on her for all the nutrients needed for growth and development.

Food Standards Agency guidelines for a healthy diet should be followed, including:

- at least five portions of fruit and vegetables per day
- foods that provide protein and iron
- starchy foods including potatoes, bread, rice and pasta
- fish at least twice a week
- dairy foods in moderation including milk, cheese and yoghurt
- only consuming sweet/processed foods in moderation.

> **The Food Standards Agency** – a government department that issues guidelines on healthy eating.

Exercise

- Being fit and healthy before conception helps the body to cope with pregnancy and birth.
- Regular exercise is needed to maintain ongoing fitness during pregnancy.
- Most forms of exercise can carry on safely during pregnancy.

> A question on diet may ask for examples of foods providing protein and iron. These include chicken, meat, fish, eggs and pulses.

Healthy weight

Being overweight:

- can affect ovulation and reduce fertility
- can interfere with the monitoring of the baby's growth and development
- can lead to health issues in pregnancy, such as high blood pressure, pre-eclampsia and diabetes
- can increase the likelihood of the mother needing a **caesarean**.

Being underweight can:

- reduce fertility, affecting periods and ovulation.

> **Caesarean** – when a baby is delivered through a surgical incision (cut) made in the mother's abdomen and uterus.

Dangers of smoking/alcohol/recreational drugs

Very serious damage can be caused to an unborn child during pregnancy by:

- smoking (including passive smoking)
- drinking alcohol
- using recreational drugs.

It is crucial to protect a foetus from these factors.

Smoking

Smoking (in men and women) can affect fertility. Once pregnant:

- chemicals from smoke inhaled by a mother will pass from her lungs into her bloodstream, then to the unborn child via the placenta
- there is a risk of premature birth, miscarriage, stillbirth and fetal abnormalities
- damage to the placenta can affect the nutrients received
- low birth weight is common
- babies may experience learning difficulties and poor growth.

Alcohol

- There is debate over how much alcohol is safe for a pregnant mother to drink.
- The more a woman drinks, the higher the risk to her baby.
- The safest approach is not to drink any alcohol.
- Regular or binge drinking is very dangerous.
- Alcohol enters the mother's bloodstream and is passed to the baby via the placenta.
- Alcohol can seriously affect the development of the baby's liver.
- The risk of premature birth and low birth weight is increased.
- Drinking heavily can cause fetal alcohol syndrome (FAS) – effects include poor growth, facial abnormalities and learning and behavioural problems.

Recreational drug use in pregnancy

- Can seriously affect an unborn baby's growth and development.
- The amount of oxygen reaching the baby can be reduced.
- There may be problems with the placenta, which can cause severe bleeding that can be life threatening for mother and baby.
- If drugs have been taken regularly, the newborn may suffer withdrawal after birth. This is very painful and distressing and requires hospitalisation.

Up-to-date immunisations

- Vaccinations contribute to a woman's health before and during pregnancy.
- This also benefits the baby.
- The whooping cough vaccine and flu vaccine are available to pregnant women.

> **Exam tip**
>
> A question on smoking may ask about the risks for children growing up in a home with smokers. The likelihood of them dying from Sudden Infant Death Syndrome is doubled. They are more at risk of asthma and chest infections, and possibly some cancers.

Now test yourself

TESTED ☐

1 State **three** factors that affect pre-conception health.
2 Explain the benefits of eating healthily in pregnancy.
3 Discuss the dangers of drinking alcohol in pregnancy.

1.3 Roles and responsibilities of parenthood

Meeting primary needs

Providing for a child's **primary needs** is a crucial part of a parent's roles and responsibilities.

Primary care needs are shown in Table 1.2.

> **Primary needs** – the basic needs that must be met in order for a child to survive.

Table 1.2 Primary care needs: roles and responsibilities of parenthood

Primary need	Parental roles/responsibilities
Food	• Providing children with adequate food and water. • Providing food that contains the right nutrients for the baby/child at each stage of development. • Providing children with regular meals and snacks to ensure they have the energy they need to grow, learn and play. • Choosing healthy food options over less healthy ones. • Making time to shop for, prepare and cook food.
Clothing	• Providing children with sufficient clothing, including clothing for all weathers. • Replacing clothes children have grown out of – which can be a considerable cost when children go through growth spurts. • Laundering and ironing clothes regularly.
Shelter	• Providing children with a safe place to live. • Ensuring the home is healthy for children to live in (e.g. is not damp, which can cause asthma/chest infections). • Making the rent or mortgage payments to ensure children have a secure home life.
Warmth	• Ensuring children are warm (e.g. by providing sufficient clothing, bedding, central heating). • Paying central heating bills. • Paying to mend the central heating system if it breaks down.
Rest/sleep	• Ensuring children get enough rest and sleep, as this is crucial to their well-being, learning, growth and development. • Parents may need to reduce their social life to ensure the child gets enough good-quality rest and sleep.

In addition, it is within a parent's roles and responsibilities to provide:

• love and nurture

• socialisation, customs, values.

Providing love and nurture

All children need and deserve to be loved and brought up in a supportive, nurturing environment.

A child who does not receive love and nurture:

- may fail to thrive
- may be unhappy and experience social and emotional difficulties, both at home and in the wider world, for example when interacting with their peers at playgroup.

A lack of love and nurture in the early years can continue to impact on children as they grow up, and the effects may even continue to be felt into adulthood.

Figure 1.3 All children need and deserve to be loved and brought up in a supportive, nurturing environment.

> **Exam tip**
>
> A question on providing love and nurture may ask how an adult who lacked a loving and nurturing role model in their own childhood may be affected. Some such adults can find it more challenging to adjust to the role of being a parent themselves, and may need additional support at this time in their lives.

Socialisation, customs and values, including patterns of behaviour, social interaction and role models

- As they grow up, children need to come to understand socially acceptable behaviour. They need to be supported in learning how to experience and manage their feelings. Parents have a responsibility to guide children in this area.
- An important part of the parental role is to be an appropriate **role model**.
- Parents will also want to give their child an understanding of their family's customs and values.
- Customs and values may be influenced by a family's religion or ethical beliefs. For example, these may include what and how a family celebrates, whether and how a family prays, what and how a family eats and the activities in which a family participates.
- The customs and values of a family are very personal, and they tend to influence a child's sense of identity. Together, these things enable a child to successfully interact socially.
- Parents need to plan opportunities for their child to socialise with their peers, to ensure that they are confident around others and are able to make friends and enjoy social times.

> **Role model** – someone who demonstrates how to behave by example.

Now test yourself

TESTED ☐

1 State the **five** key primary care needs of a child.
2 Discuss how the quality of shelter provided for a child may impact on their health and well-being.
3 Explain why sufficient rest/sleep is important for children.
4 Discuss how parents may provide for their child's socialisation needs.

1.4 Recognise and evaluate methods of contraception, their efficiency and reliability

There are many factors for couples to consider when choosing an appropriate method of contraception.

Barrier methods

Male condoms

- Sheath made from latex or polyurethane.
- Put onto the erect penis before it comes into contact with the vagina.
- Sex is interrupted in order to put one on.
- 98 per cent effective if used correctly.
- Helps to protect against many STIs (sexually transmitted infections).
- If used incorrectly, it can come off or split, making it ineffective.
- Widely available from chemists, supermarkets, etc.
- Discarded after one use.
- Allows the man to take responsibility for contraception.

> **Barrier method** – a method of contraception in which a device or preparation prevents sperm from reaching an egg.

Female condoms

- Sheath made from polyurethane.
- Put inside the vagina before it comes into contact with the penis.
- Sex is interrupted in order to put one in.
- 95 per cent effective if used correctly.
- Helps to protect against many STIs.
- Possible for the condom to be pushed too far into the vagina.
- Widely available in chemists and supermarkets.
- More expensive than male condoms.

> **Exam tip**
>
> In a question about contraception, you may be asked which contraceptives can be obtained for free. Male condoms are free from family planning clinics; female condoms often are too.

Diaphragm or cap

- Dome-shaped piece of latex/silicone that covers the cervix.
- Inserted into the vagina before sex. Used alongside spermicidal gel/cream (to kill sperm).
- Can be inserted into the vagina a few hours before sex, so need not interrupt sex.
- Reusable. Must be removed and washed after intercourse.
- 92 per cent effective if used correctly.
- Helps to protect against some STIs.
- Women can have difficulty learning how to use them.
- Can cause cystitis (infection of the urinary tract).

Contraceptive pill

The contraceptive pill is a **hormonal method** of contraception for women that comes in two forms:

- combined pill
- progestogen-only pill.

> **Hormonal method** – a method of contraception in which hormones prevent eggs from being released from the ovaries, thicken cervical mucus to prevent sperm from entering the uterus, and thin the lining of the uterus to prevent implantation.

Combined pill

- Contains hormones that prevent pregnancy.
- A woman takes the pill for 21 days. She then has a break for 7 days, within which she has a period. Then the cycle repeats.
- Needs to be taken regularly at the same time of day.
- 99 per cent effective if used correctly.
- A woman can still become pregnant if she forgets to take it, vomits after taking it or has severe diarrhoea.
- Can help women with heavy/painful periods.
- May help to protect against some cancers.
- Possible side-effects include weight gain, headaches, mood swings, depression, raised blood pressure and, uncommonly, blood clots.
- Method does not interrupt sex.

Progestogen-only pill

- Contains progestogen hormone only, which prevents pregnancy.
- Taken every day within a specified three-hour period.
- 99 per cent effective if used correctly.
- A woman can still become pregnant if she forgets to take it, vomits after taking it, has severe diarrhoea or takes certain medication.
- Women who cannot take oestrogen may be able to take it.
- Side-effects can include spot-prone skin, tender breasts, and irregular periods.
- Method does not interrupt sex.

Intrauterine device/system (IUD or IUS)

- Small, t-shaped plastic device that is inserted into the uterus by a doctor/ nurse. Releases the progestogen hormone, preventing pregnancy.
- 99 per cent effective, for five years or three years, depending on the type, if used correctly.
- The couple do not need to think about contraception every day or whenever they have sex.
- May make periods lighter/shorter/stop, so can help women with heavy/ painful periods.
- Can be used by women who cannot take the combined pill.
- Possible side-effects include mood swings, skin problems, breast tenderness, getting an infection after it is inserted.
- Insertion can be uncomfortable.
- Does not protect against STIs.

Contraceptive injection

- Woman injected every few weeks (often every 12 weeks) with a hormone that prevents pregnancy.
- Can be a suitable choice for women who find it difficult to take a tablet at the same time daily.
- 99 per cent effective if used correctly.
- Can protect against some cancers and infections.
- Side-effects can include headaches, tender breasts, weight gain, mood swings and irregular periods.
- After stopping injections, it can take up to a year before fertility levels return to normal.
- Method does not interrupt sex.

Contraceptive patch

- Worn on the skin.
- Introduces hormones to the body, preventing pregnancy.
- 99 per cent effective if used correctly.
- May protect against some cancers and infections.
- Still effective if the woman vomits or has severe diarrhoea.
- Side-effects can include headaches and raised blood pressure, and uncommonly, blood clots.
- Patch must be changed each week for three weeks then there is a week off.
- Method does not interrupt sex.

Contraceptive implant

- Health professional inserts a small flexible tube into the skin of a woman's upper arm.
- It releases the progestogen hormone, preventing pregnancy.
- 99 per cent effective if used correctly for three years, after which time it is removed.
- The couple do not need to think about contraception every day or whenever they have sex.
- Some medicines may make it ineffective.
- Possible side-effects include swelling, tenderness or bruising after insertion, periods may change.
- Does not protect against STIs.

Natural family planning

- A woman records the symptoms in her body (by taking her temperature and monitoring her vaginal secretions, for example) that indicate when she is fertile and able to conceive – around eight days in each month.
- On other days, she will be able to have sex without conceiving.
- On fertile days, a condom can be used, or the couple can abstain (not have sex).
- This method is compatible with all cultures and faiths (some do not permit the use of contraception).
- Up to 98 per cent effective if used correctly.
- Takes time to identify the fertile days.
- No protection against STIs.
- No side-effects or costs.

In another natural contraceptive measure, the man withdraws his penis from the vagina before he ejaculates semen into it. However:

- Semen can be released before ejaculation, so this is an unreliable measure.
- This can be frustrating for both partners.

Emergency contraceptive pill

- Prevents pregnancy after a woman has had unprotected sex, or if she thinks that the method of conception used has failed.
- Must be taken within 72 hours of unprotected sex, but the sooner it is taken the better.
- If taken within 24 hours, it is up to 98 per cent effective.
- Effectiveness decreases over time – after 72 hours it is 52 per cent effective.
- Can be bought from a pharmacy (by those aged 16 years and over).
- It is free of charge from some GP surgeries, family planning/sexual health clinics, NHS walk-in centres and hospitals.

Now test yourself

TESTED ☐

1 Outline the choices available for couples seeking to use barrier methods of contraception.
2 Discuss the choices available for couples seeking to use hormone methods of contraception.
3 Explain the most reliable natural family planning method.

1.4 Recognise and evaluate methods of contraception, their efficiency and reliability

1.5 The structure and function of male and female reproductive systems

To understand how reproduction happens, you need to understand the male and female reproductive systems.

Female reproductive system

This includes:

Ovaries

- Two ovaries control the production of the female reproductive hormones, oestrogen and progesterone.
- These hormones govern the development of the female body and the menstrual cycle.
- Within the ovaries are undeveloped egg cells called ova (one cell is called an ovum).

Fallopian tubes

- Connect the ovaries to the uterus.
- Lined by minute hairs called cilia.
- Each month, one of the ovaries releases an egg into a tube (the fallopian tube), and the hairs help the egg to reach the uterus by wafting it along the tube.

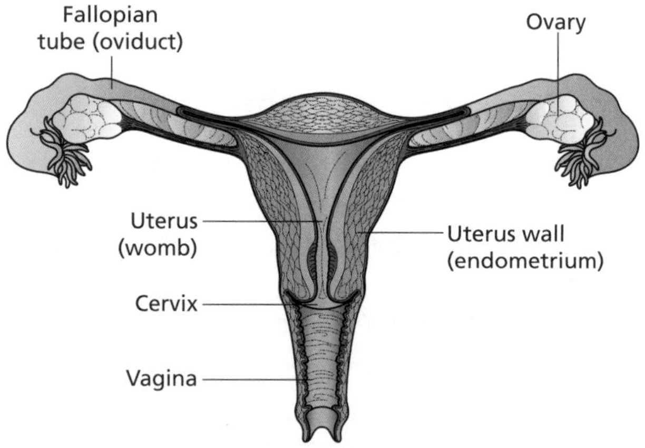

Uterus/lining of the uterus

- The uterus is the hollow, pear-shaped muscular bag where an unborn child grows and develops.
- The lining of the uterus is soft.
- It is here that an egg will become implanted.

Cervix

- A very strong ring of muscles between the uterus and vagina.
- It is usually closed.
- Keeps the baby securely in place in the womb throughout pregnancy.
- The cervix dilates (opens) during labour to allow the baby to be born.

Vagina

- Muscular tube that leads downwards, connecting the cervix to the outside of the body.
- Where the man's penis enters the body during sex.
- Folds of skin called labia meet at the entrance of the vagina, forming the vulva.
- The urethra, through which urine passes, opens into the vulva but is separate from the vagina.

The menstrual cycle

- The cycle in which women have their periods and are fertile (can conceive a baby).

Figure 1.4 Female reproductive system

Common mistake

Thinking the uterus and the womb are two separate body parts. Remember that the uterus is sometimes called the womb.

- Girls begin their periods when they become sexually mature (average age = 12 years) and they continue until menopause (average age = 51 years).
- Women experience periods differently, but menstruation (a period) generally lasts three to seven days (average = five days).
- During menstruation, blood flows from the uterus and leaves the body via the vagina.
- A new egg then develops in one of the ovaries.
- About 14 days after the first day of menstruation, the egg is released from the ovary and travels along the fallopian tube to the uterus.
- The lining of the uterus will be thickened and ready to receive an egg fertilised by sperm.
- If this occurs, and the fertilised egg implants in the womb lining, the baby will start to grow.
- If implantation of a fertilised egg does not occur by the end of the menstrual cycle, the blood, uterus lining and egg are flushed out via another period and the cycle begins again.

Revision activity

Try copying the female reproductive system diagram onto a piece of paper. It may help you to remember the names and positions of the body parts.

Male reproductive system

This includes:

Testes

- The scrotum is a bag of skin that contains two testes.
- These make millions of sperm – the male sex cells.
- They also produce hormones, including testosterone, which governs the development of the male body.

Sperm duct system/epididymis

The sperm duct system consists of:

- the epididymis, which contains the sperm
- the vas deferens, which are the sperm ducts (tubes) that sperm pass through
- glands that produce nutrient-rich fluid – called semen – which mixes with the sperm and carries it.

Urethra

- The tube inside the penis carrying both urine and semen, but not both at the same time.
- A ring of muscle controls this.

Penis

The penis consists of:

- the shaft (the main part that goes inside the vagina)
- the glans (the tip), which has a small opening.

Through this opening, sperm and urine leave the body (separately) via the urethra.

Vas deferens

- This is a muscular tube that extends upwards from the testicles.
- It transfers sperm that contains semen to the urethra.

How reproduction takes place

- Reproduction occurs when a sperm cell combines with an egg cell to produce a fertilised egg cell.
- The egg can be fertilised (combined with a sperm cell) after a woman ovulates.
- If the fertilised egg implants in the womb lining, the woman becomes pregnant.

Ovulation

- Occurs when an egg is released from one of the ovaries and travels along the fallopian tube, around day 14 of the menstrual cycle.
- A jelly-like coating ensures that the egg does not stick to the sides of the tubes.
- It is moved along the fallopian tube by the cilia (hair-like structures inside the fallopian tube).

Conception/fertilisation

- Occurs when a sperm penetrates an egg following ejaculation of sperm from the penis into the vagina.
- On passing through the cervix and uterus, the sperm meets the egg in the fallopian tubes and loses its tail.
- The egg and sperm then fuse as one cell.
- The fertilised egg continues along the fallopian tubes.
- Four to five days later, the fertilised egg is a mass of around 16 cells.
- This forms a ball of tissue (the blastocyst).

Implantation

- After around another seven days, the fertilised egg reaches the uterus.
- It implants itself in the enriched lining.
- Once firmly attached conception has been achieved.
- The egg is now called an embryo.
- Its outer cells link with the mother's blood supply, forming the baby's support system – the **umbilical cord**, **amnion** and **placenta** (via which it will receive nutrients from the mother).

Development of the embryo

The development of the embryo is shown in Figure 1.5.

Development of the foetus

The development of the foetus is shown in Figure 1.6.

Exam tip

You may be asked to give a timeline explaining how long conception/fertilisation and implantation take.

Umbilical cord – flexible cord-like structure that connects the baby to the mother's placenta while in the womb.

Amnion – closed sac in which the baby develops in the womb; contains amniotic fluid.

Placenta – flat, round organ in the womb of a pregnant woman that supplies the baby with all the oxygen, food and nutrients it needs.

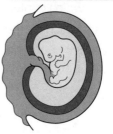

Embryo 6–7 weeks

Figure 1.5 Development of the embryo

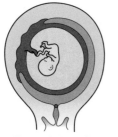
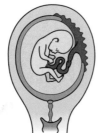
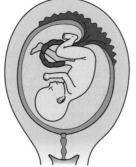

Foetus 8–9 weeks Foetus 10–14 weeks Foetus 15–22 weeks Foetus 23–30 weeks Foetus 31–40 weeks

Figure 1.6 Development of the foetus

Multiple pregnancies

- A multiple pregnancy is when more than one baby grows in the uterus.
- Identical twins are the result of one fertilised egg dividing into two cells.
- Non-identical twins are the result of two separate eggs being released and fertilised by two different sperm.

The signs and symptoms of pregnancy

There are some common signs and symptoms of pregnancy, but not all women will have all of the symptoms. Women experience signs and symptoms at different rates.

Therefore, some women will be further along in the pregnancy than others when they discover that they are pregnant.

Exam tip

Remember that a missed period is only a reliable sign of pregnancy for women who usually have a regular monthly menstrual cycle.

Missed period

- The first sign of pregnancy is often a missed period, or a very light period.
- This is generally the most reliable sign of pregnancy.

Breast changes

- The breasts may feel similar to just before a period, becoming larger and feeling tender.
- Some women may feel tingling and veins may be more visible.
- The nipples may appear darker and stand out.

Passing urine frequently

- Pregnant women often need to pass urine more frequently.
- There may also be constipation and an increase of vaginal discharge without any soreness or irritation.

Tiredness

- Women may feel tired or exhausted, particularly during the first 12 weeks of pregnancy.
- This is due to hormonal changes in the body.
- These changes can also cause a woman to feel emotional and upset at this time.

Nausea

- Pregnant women may feel sick and nauseous and/or vomit. This is often called 'morning sickness', but it can occur at any time of day.
- This symptom generally begins around six weeks after a pregnant woman's last period.

Figure 1.7 Pregnancy usually begins to show with a 'baby bump' at around 12–16 weeks.

Now test yourself

TESTED

1 Explain the function of a woman's ovaries in reproduction.
2 In the male reproductive system, explain the function of the sperm duct system/epididymis.
3 Outline how identical twins are conceived.
4 Outline how non-identical twins are conceived.
5 Name **five** signs and symptoms of pregnancy.

LO2: Understand antenatal care and preparation for birth

Antenatal care is the care given to a pregnant mother and her unborn baby during pregnancy and ahead of the birth. Some aspects of antenatal care also extend to the father or the mother's partner.

2.1 The roles of the different health professionals supporting the pregnant mother

> **Antenatal care** – the care received by a woman during her pregnancy.
>
> **Postnatal care** – the care received by a woman following the birth of her baby.

REVISED

A pregnant mother will be supported by a diverse team of health professionals, as shown in Figure 2.1.

Midwife

- Midwives are experts in normal pregnancy and birth.
- They look after a pregnant woman and her baby throughout the phase of antenatal care, during labour and birth, and for up to 28 days after the baby has been born.

The responsibilities of midwives include:

- providing full antenatal care, including parenting classes, clinical examinations and screening
- identifying high-risk pregnancies
- monitoring women and supporting them during labour and the birthing process
- teaching new and expectant mothers how to feed, care for and bathe their babies
- checking a healthy baby over before it leaves hospital.

Midwives fall into three categories:

1: Hospital midwives

These midwives are based in:

- a hospital, a birth centre or midwife-led unit
- antenatal clinics, and on the labour ward and **postnatal** wards.

2: Community midwives

- Visit pregnant women at home or at a specialised clinic. (Clinics may also be found within children's centres and GP surgeries.)
- They also attend home births.
- They are responsible for the provision of **postnatal care** for both home births and hospital births.
- They will visit new mothers at home after the birth for up to ten days.

Midwifery services are increasingly moving from hospitals to the community.

Figure 2.1 Health professionals who support the pregnant mother

> **Exam tip**
>
> Remember that a normal birth is a vaginal birth without the need for interventions.

> **Postnatal** – relating to or denoting the period after the birth of a baby.

Figure 2.2 Community midwives visit new mothers at home after the birth.

3: Independent midwives

- Work privately, outside of the NHS.
- Most likely to work with women intending to have a home birth.

Obstetrician

An obstetrician takes on the antenatal care of mothers for whom there is a complication. This can be in response to:

- a pre-existing acute or chronic medical condition in the mother that complicates the pregnancy and/or birth
- a complication with the mother or baby identified during pregnancy that complicates the pregnancy and/or birth
- a baby becoming distressed during labour.

An obstetrician's role includes assisting delivery and performing caesarean sections.

General practitioner

The general practitioner (GP):

- is generally, a mother's first port of call following a positive home pregnancy test
- confirms pregnancy and books the mother into the 'maternity system' so that appointments for scans and check-ups are triggered.

The GP's role also includes:

- answering the mother's questions
- discussing relevant issues (for example, mother's existing medical conditions)
- making necessary referrals to other professionals
- treating the mother for non-pregnancy related medical problems during pregnancy
- responding to emergency concerns relating to the pregnancy (for example, abdominal pain)
- potentially being involved in the delivery of babies in GP-led units
- providing postnatal medical care.

Revision activity

If you find the titles of medical professionals difficult to spell or remember, try writing them out a few times.

Gynaecologist

- Specialist in the female reproductive organs and the ability to reproduce.
- Treats fertility conditions and early pregnancy symptoms.

Their role includes:

- care of mothers with complicated medical problems
- emergency care for problems in early pregnancy (for example, bleeding)
- termination of a pregnancy, including pre-assessment and counselling.

Paediatrician

- A paediatrician is a doctor specialising in babies and children.
- They may be present at the birth if there is a concern about a baby's health.
- If there is an unexpected concern following the birth, a paediatrician is likely to be called.
- They may check a healthy baby over before it leaves hospital.

Common mistake

Thinking that only a paediatrician checks a healthy baby over before it leaves hospital. A midwife trained in the appropriate specialised area of care may also undertake this task.

Now test yourself

TESTED ☐

1 Explain the three categories of midwife.
2 Outline the key responsibilities of a gynaecologist.
3 Outline the key responsibilities of a paediatrician.

2.2 The importance of antenatal and parenting classes

- Antenatal and parenting classes help with preparation for a safe pregnancy, labour and parenthood.
- Expectant mothers and their partners usually attended classes weekly from around weeks 30–32 of pregnancy.
- Those expecting twins will generally begin classes in week 24 of pregnancy, as the babies are more likely to be born early.
- Classes are generally informal and fun.
- There are local differences in provision. For example, some areas may offer two separate classes – one focusing on pregnancy, labour and birth, and another focusing on parenthood and baby care.

Preparing for a safe pregnancy and delivery

Antenatal and parenting classes help with preparing for a safe pregnancy and delivery by:

- providing advice on staying fit and healthy during pregnancy through safe exercise and a healthy diet
- explaining the various arrangements for labour and birth – this information helps a mother to create a personal birth plan and to discuss this with professionals
- giving mothers the chance to talk over any concerns, and perhaps meet key professionals who will care for them during labour.

Preparation of both parents for labour and parenthood

Antenatal and parenting classes usually help to prepare both parents for labour and parenthood by giving information about:

- what happens during labour and birth, and how to cope
- types of pain relief and relaxation methods (for example, breathing techniques)
- types of birth (for example, home birth, hospital birth)
- different types of birth interventions, such as ventouse or forceps delivery (see page 34)
- caring for a baby (for example, feeding, sleeping, bathing)
- the mother's health after the birth.

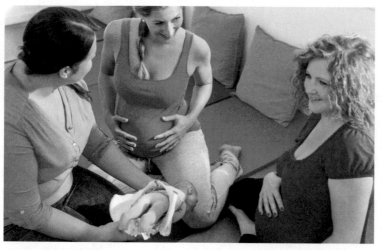

Figure 2.3 Antenatal and parenting classes help a mother to prepare for the birth.

Role of the father/partner in supporting the mother throughout pregnancy and birth

The father/partner will learn how to support the mother throughout pregnancy during antenatal and parenting classes. This includes:

- providing practical support with tasks if she is feeling tired
- being emotionally supportive if she is anxious about coping with birth.

They will also learn how to help the mother during labour and birth by:

- massaging her back, shoulders or legs
- supporting her body
- timing contractions
- giving encouragement, drinks, snacks or ice cubes
- sponging her down
- talking/finding ways to pass the time
- helping her to find a comfortable position
- making sure health professionals are aware of the birthing plan
- learning relaxation and breathing techniques alongside the mother and participating alongside her during labour and birth.

For the birth to be an emotionally satisfying experience

Antenatal and parenting classes focus on making the birth an emotionally satisfying experience by:

- enabling discussion of emotions and feelings during pregnancy, birth and after the birth, so that parents have realistic expectations
- enabling the creation of a personalised birth plan
- enabling the father/partner to plan how they will participate in the birth and support the mother
- providing refresher classes for those who have already had a baby
- providing information about the sources of support.

> **Revision activity**
>
> Think about how a first-time mother might be feeling about the prospect of giving birth. Write three sentences about this.

Promotion of healthy lifestyle and breastfeeding

Promotion of a healthy lifestyle is a key part of antenatal classes. Parents will learn about:

- diet and exercise
- the negative impact of smoking, alcohol and recreational drugs during pregnancy and after the birth
- the many benefits of breastfeeding (see page 50).

Now test yourself

TESTED ☐

1 Explain the importance of attending antenatal classes.
2 Outline the role of the father/partner in supporting the mother throughout pregnancy and birth.
3 Identify **three** things that will be covered when a healthy lifestyle is promoted at antenatal classes.

2.3 Routine checks carried out at an antenatal clinic, including scans

The first antenatal appointment occurs at week 8 of pregnancy. The midwife:

- carries out routine checks (see below); these will be repeated on later visits, to monitor the health of mother and baby
- asks questions about medical history
- organises an ultrasound dating scan appointment (see below).

Weight check

- Women are weighed to establish a baseline weight.
- Their weight can then be tracked throughout pregnancy.
- If a pregnant woman gains more weight than expected, it could be a sign of **pre-eclampsia**, in which case treatment will be needed.
- Weight loss could indicate illness in the mother, or that the baby has stopped growing.

Blood tests

These are carried out to check for:

- Anaemia – a lack of iron leading to tiredness and listlessness. Folic acid and iron tablets may be needed.
- High blood sugar – this reveals if the mother has diabetes. Diabetes can develop during pregnancy and stop afterwards.
- Blood group – in case a blood transfusion is needed later. This can occur if the mother bleeds excessively.
- German measles (rubella) – this will reveal whether the woman is immune to this dangerous disease for the developing unborn baby, which can cause brain damage, deafness and blindness.
- **Hepatitis B and C** – without treatment, these can cause liver disease.
- **HIV** – this can be passed from mother to baby via the placenta in pregnancy or via breastfeeding after birth.

Blood pressure (BP)

- A baseline BP measurement is taken.
- The average healthy BP range for a mother under 35 years is 110/70–120/80.
- Blood pressure above 140/90 can indicate pre-eclampsia.

Urine test

This can reveal potential problems during pregnancy:

- Protein in the urine might be the result of an infection. It can also indicate the onset of a serious condition such as pre-eclampsia.
- Glucose (sugar) in the urine can indicate diabetes, which can be controlled by diet/insulin.
- **Ketones** might be present if there has been excessive vomiting (hyperemesis). Hospitalisation is needed. Without treatment, a serious condition called ketosis can occur, which can be life-threatening.

> **Pre-eclampsia** – a condition in which a woman has high levels of protein in her urine. Swelling in the feet, legs and hands is also common. If left untreated, eclampsia can develop, which can be very harmful to mother and baby. Symptoms of eclampsia include seizures in the mother.

> **Hepatitis** – virus that can cause liver disease. There are five 'types' of viral hepatitis – A, B, C, D and E.
>
> **HIV** – human immunodeficiency virus. It is spread through bodily fluids, and attacks the body's immune system, weakening the ability to fight everyday illnesses.

> **Ketones** – produced when the body burns fat for energy. They are also produced when someone loses weight or when the body is lacking the sufficient insulin to use sugar for energy.

STIs

Sexually transmitted infections:

- can be harmful for an unborn baby
- can be pre-existing, or caught during pregnancy
- can be more serious when caught during pregnancy, and even life-threatening for the mother/baby.

Some STIs, including chlamydia and gonorrhoea, can be treated and cured with antibiotics. STIs caused by viruses, such as genital herpes, hepatitis B and HIV, cannot be cured. These conditions may be treated to reduce the risk of them being passed to the baby.

Examination of the uterus

Examination of the uterus is performed throughout pregnancy. A gloved index and middle finger is inserted into the vagina up to the cervix to assess:

- how soft the cervix is
- whether there is any thinning or opening of the cervix
- the position of the cervix, whether posterior (facing the tailbone) or anterior (facing the front)
- how far into the pelvis the baby has descended
- which way the baby is facing (presentation).

Baby's heartbeat

- This is checked and monitored to confirm that the baby is alive.
- The midwife/doctor will also listen to hear if the heartbeat is normal.
- The expected heartbeat of an unborn baby is 110–160 beats per minute.

Ultrasound dating scan

Around weeks 8–14 of pregnancy, an ultrasound dating scan is carried out by a sonographer. This checks:

- how far along the pregnancy is, so a due date can be calculated
- the baby's development
- whether more than one baby is expected
- that the baby is growing in the right place
- for abnormalities, as some may be detected at this early stage.

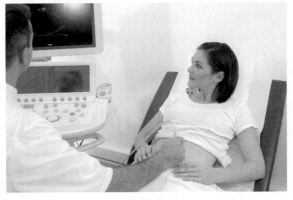

Figure 2.4 An ultrasound dating scan is carried out by a sonographer.

TESTED

Now test yourself

1 Explain why checking for STIs is important.
2 Outline the checks made at an ultrasound dating scan.
3 Identify **three** checks that are made during an examination of the uterus.

2.4 Specialised diagnostic tests

A number of these are offered during pregnancy.

Ultrasound anomaly scan/mid-pregnancy scan

- Carried out in weeks 18–21 of pregnancy.
- Checks for major physical abnormalities in the baby.
- Cannot find everything that might be wrong.

Exam tip

Remember: most babies will develop normally. However, when serious problems are identified, babies may need treatment/surgery after birth. In rare cases, no treatment is possible, and the baby will die during pregnancy or soon after birth.

Table 2.1 The ultrasound anomaly scan/mid-pregnancy scan

The scan looks at the baby's:	11 conditions are looked for:
<ul><li>bones</li><li>heart</li><li>brain</li><li>spinal cord</li><li>face</li><li>kidneys</li><li>abdomen.</li></ul>	<ul><li>anencephaly</li><li>open spina bifida</li><li>cleft lip</li><li>diaphragmatic hernia</li><li>gastrochisis</li><li>exomphalos</li><li>serious cardiac abnormalities</li><li>bilateral renal agenesis</li><li>lethal skeletal dysplasia</li><li>Edwards' syndrome, or t18</li><li>Patau's syndrome, or t13.</li></ul>

Nuchal fold translucency (NT) test

- The amount of fluid present under the skin at the back of the unborn baby's neck is measured.
- Babies with Down's syndrome often have an increased amount of this fluid.
- Pregnant women are offered this test between weeks 11 and 13 of pregnancy.
- Screening estimates the level of risk, but cannot determine whether a baby definitely has Down's syndrome.
- Other tests can accurately diagnose it, but these carry a small risk of miscarriage.
- This screening test will indicate whether a diagnostic test should be offered.
- Not all mothers will choose to have the NT test/further diagnostic test.

Alpha fetoprotein (AFP) test

- AFP is made in the liver of an unborn baby.
- This blood test checks the level of AFP in the mother's blood – where traces of the baby's AFP are found.
- This shows whether a baby might have a condition such as spina bifida or anencephaly.

Chorionic villus sampling (CVS)

- Checks for genetic disorders (for example, Down's syndrome).
- Carried out between weeks 11 and 14 of pregnancy.
- Cells are removed from the placenta via a needle inserted through the mother's abdomen, or a tube (or small forceps) inserted through the cervix.

- Only offered when there is a high risk of a baby having a genetic condition, i.e. if:
  - an antenatal screening test has indicated a problem
  - the mother has had a previous pregnancy with these problems
  - there is family history of a genetic condition.

Risks of CVS

- Carries a risk of miscarriage (1–2 per cent) and infection. For this reason not all mothers offered the test decide to go ahead.
- There is no cure for the majority of conditions detected.
- If a serious disorder is detected, the implications will be fully discussed. The mother may choose to continue with the pregnancy knowing the condition her baby will be born with or she may consider a termination.

Amniocentesis

- Carried out between weeks 15 and 18 of pregnancy.
- A small sample of **amniotic fluid** is removed and tested.
- This tests for genetic disorders.
- May be offered as an alternative to CVS (and in the same circumstances).

> **Amniotic fluid** – the fluid that surrounds the baby in the womb.

Risks of amniocentesis

- Risk of causing miscarriage is slightly reduced compared with CVS.
- Results cannot be given until a later stage of pregnancy.
- This has implications for the possibility of terminating the pregnancy later on if a problem is found (the normal deadline for termination of a pregnancy is 24 weeks).

Non-invasive prenatal testing (NIPT) blood test

- A screening test that assesses the likelihood of having a baby with Down's syndrome, Edwards' syndrome or Patau's syndrome.
- Carried out from week 10 of pregnancy.
- More accurate and does not carry a risk of miscarriage.
- A blood sample is taken from the mother.
- Fragments of the baby's DNA within this are analysed for possible **chromosomal abnormalities**.
- If the risk of abnormality is high, a diagnostic test such as CVS or amniocentesis will be offered.
- NHS hospitals do not generally offer NIPT. Therefore, most parents wanting the test will need to pay to have it done privately.
- Some choose to have NIPT before deciding to have a diagnostic test that carries a risk of miscarriage.
- When a high-risk NIPT result is given, it is likely that the diagnostic test will also be positive.
- If the NIPT is negative, the parents may decide against a diagnostic test.

> **Chromosomal abnormalities** – occur when a portion of chromosomal DNA is irregular, missing or duplicated.

Now test yourself

TESTED

1 What is an ultrasound scan?
2 Outline the purpose of **two** different diagnostic tests that are offered during pregnancy.
3 Explain why a mother may choose not to have a CVS test.

2.5 The choices available for delivery

- Several choices are available for delivery and birth (see Figure 2.5).
- The GP normally explains the options.
- The mother can talk these over with her midwife/antenatal class leader.

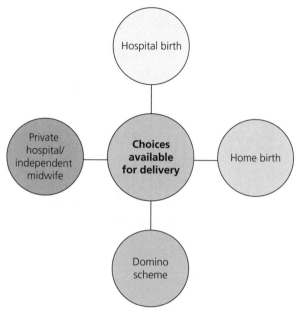

Figure 2.5 The choices available for delivery

Common mistake

Assuming that all of the provision will be available within one local area. For example, some mothers may have a consultant-led unit nearby, while others may have a midwife- or GP-led unit.

Hospital birth

Types of hospital provision can include:

- consultant-led units
- midwife- or GP-led units
- birthing centres (generally most homely).

Within birthing centres:

- delivery rooms are increasingly home-like and comfortable
- soft chairs and beanbags enable mothers to change position, helping pain management
- warm baths and showers may also be available to soothe pain.

Maternity units increasingly offer birthing pools for comfort and pain relief, which also enable a water birth if labour progresses normally.

Advantages of hospital births include:

- Highly trained staff and equipment are available in emergencies – this could save a baby's life and is reassuring.
- Some pain relief can only be given in hospital.
- Forceps, ventouse and caesarean section deliveries (see page 34) can only be carried out in hospital.
- Midwives are on hand after the birth to help with issues such as feeding – this means they can let a mother rest by taking a baby into the nursery.
- The demands of home life are left behind.

Home birth

Home birth is an option when:

- pregnancy is normal
- mother and baby are well.

A midwife attends during labour. If labour does not progress normally or the mother needs help, the midwife arranges a transfer to hospital.

Advantages of a home birth include:

- It occurs in familiar, relaxing surroundings.
- Labour is not interrupted by travelling to hospital.
- Older siblings can stay with the mother and can be involved in labour/ birth.
- The mother is more likely to be looked after by a midwife she knows.
- Interventions such as forceps or ventouse are less likely.

The NHS report that for women having their second or subsequent baby, a planned home birth is as safe as having a baby in a hospital or midwife-led unit. However, for women having their first baby, home birth slightly increases the risk of a poor outcome for the baby.

Other considerations with deciding to have a home birth:

- Transfer to hospital may be needed.
- Poor outcomes include death of the baby and problems that might affect the baby's quality of life.
- Epidurals (pain relief) are not given at home.
- The midwife/doctor might advise that a hospital birth is safer in some circumstances.

Domino scheme

- Community midwives provide antenatal care then meet the mother at the hospital for the delivery.
- This scheme is followed by some hospitals.
- The midwife is often able to assess the mother closely during labour, so the move to hospital will not be made until close to the delivery.
- If all is well, the mother and baby will be able to leave hospital after six hours, shortening the hospital stay.

Private hospital/independent midwife

- Some parents pay for these, rather than accessing free NHS provision.
- Parents who can afford it may decide to pay because they feel that the standard of the provision is higher.
- A private hospital is also a popular choice for families in the public eye.
- An independent midwife might not undertake all of the responsibilities of NHS midwives, so mothers may in fact use both services.

Revision activity

Watch the video at www.nhs.uk/conditions/pregnancy-and-baby/pages/where-can-i-give-birth.aspx

Now test yourself

TESTED

1 Outline the choices available for the delivery.
2 Explain why some parents may pay for a private hospital.
3 Explain the advantages of a hospital birth.

2.6 The stages of labour and the methods of delivery, including pain relief

REVISED

Every labour is different, but all pass through three common stages.

Stage one – neck of the uterus opens

Signs that labour is beginning include:

- The uterus muscles start to contract and release. These contractions gradually become stronger and occur closer together.
- The 'waters break' – the bag of amniotic fluid around the baby bursts, causing anything from a trickle to a gush of liquid from the vagina. When the waters break it is time to go to hospital (or chosen birth option) because there is a risk of infection for the baby.
- The woman has a 'show' – this is when a plug of mucus that has sealed off the uterus during pregnancy comes away from the cervix as it dilates (gets wider). This will be stained with blood, but no blood should be lost. Not all women experience a show, but it can occur.

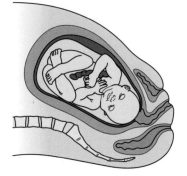

Figure 2.6 The first stage of labour

As the neck of the uterus continues to open:

- More pain relief is required as the contractions become stronger, more regular and longer lasting. A warm bath can help.
- Mothers are encouraged to move around in an upright position.
- The cervix gradually dilates to 8–10 cm wide.
- If the head of the baby is not already engaged in the mother's pelvis, it will move into position.
- As the end of this stage approaches, intense contractions can cause the mother to feel agitated, vomit, sweat or shiver. Due to pressure from the baby's head, she may lose bladder and/or bowel control.
- When contractions get even closer together, stronger and more intense, the mother enters the **transition stage** that leads into the second stage of labour.

> **Transition stage** – this links the end of the first stage of labour and the beginning of the second stage of labour.

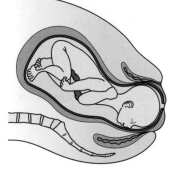

Figure 2.7 Diagram of a baby with the head engaged

Stage two – the birth of the baby

- Starts when the cervix becomes fully dilated at 10 cm.
- Ends when the baby has been born.
- The vagina and the open cervix now form a single passage known as the birth canal.
- The head of the baby moves into the birth canal.
- The mother begins to push with each contraction, to help move the baby down the birth canal.
- This can be exhausting, so she will need to rest between contractions.
- When the baby's head can be seen (crowning), the mother stops pushing so that the head is born gradually and safely. Instead, the mother pants or blows out, to control her breathing.
- The head must be born slowly to avoid the mother's skin tearing between the vagina and rectum (the perineum).
- A cut (an episiotomy) may need to be made if the perineum does not stretch enough.
- The hard work of labour is over once the head has been born, as the body can be turned so that the shoulders are delivered one at a time.
- The rest of the baby's body, which slides out easily, follows.
- If the baby needs mucus removing from its airways or to be given oxygen, this can be done as soon as the head is born, before the rest of the body is delivered.
- The umbilical cord is clamped and cut. The father/partner might cut the cord.
- The baby is generally placed on the mother for skin-to-skin contact.
- Some blood from the birth and a protective layer of oily vernix (see page 39) are likely to be present on the baby's skin.

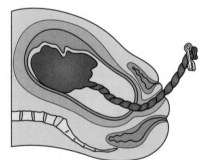

Figure 2.8 The second stage of labour

Stage three – delivery of placenta and membranes

In the shortest stage of labour, which follows the birth:

- Contractions begin again and these push the placenta out.
- An injection of the hormone syntocinon may be given, to stimulate contractions and speed up the process. This helps to prevent the loss of blood and is helpful if the mother is exhausted.
- If a tear occurred in the perineum or a cut was made, it will be sewed up under local anaesthetic.

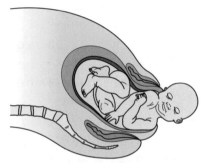

Figure 2.9 The third stage of labour

Methods of delivery

There are various methods of delivery. Some are planned in advance. Others become necessary should help be needed during labour.

The NHS reports that about one in eight women has an assisted birth, where forceps or a ventouse suction cup are used to help deliver baby's head. This can be because:

- there are concerns about the baby's heart rate
- the baby is in an awkward position
- the mother is too exhausted.

The procedures are safe but are only used when necessary.

Forceps

- Forceps look similar to tongs – a curved metal instrument that fits around baby's head.
- They are carefully positioned around the baby's head, then joined together at the handles.
- As the mother pushes with a contraction, an obstetrician gently pulls to help deliver the baby.
- Some forceps are designed to turn the baby to the right position to be born.
- Forceps are usually more successful than ventouse, but are more likely to result in vaginal tearing.

Ventouse

- A ventouse (vacuum extractor) is a plastic or metal cup that fits firmly on the baby's head and is attached by suction.
- As the mother pushes with a contraction, an obstetrician gently pulls to help deliver the baby.
- The process leaves a small swelling on baby's head, which will disappear quickly.
- The cup may also leave a temporary bruise.
- A ventouse is not used with babies born before week 34 of pregnancy because the head is too soft.

Elective/emergency caesarean section

- This is an operation to deliver a baby through a cut made in the abdomen and womb.
- It may be recommended as an elective (planned) procedure or it may be done in an emergency, if a vaginal birth becomes unsafe.
- Caesareans are a major operation and there are risks, so they are not suitable for every mother.

Reasons for a caesarean include:

- the baby being in the breech position (feet first)
- a low-lying placenta (placenta praevia)
- pre-eclampsia
- infections such as STIs and untreated HIV
- the baby not getting enough oxygen and nutrients so needs to be delivered immediately
- labour is not progressing
- excessive vaginal bleeding.

www.hoddereducation.co.uk/myrevisionnotes

Pain relief

It is natural for mothers to be concerned about handling the pain of childbirth, so it is important that they include the options for pain relief in their birth plan.

Gas and air (Entonox)

- This mixture of oxygen and nitrous oxide gas does not remove all pain, but it helps to reduce it.
- Mothers breathe in the gas and air through a mask or mouthpiece, which they hold themselves. This gives them a sense of control.
- It works within about 20 seconds, so a deep slow breath will be taken as a contraction begins.
- There may be a light-headed sensation. Some mothers stop using it, as they may feel sick, sleepy or unable to concentrate.
- A painkilling injection can be given alongside.

Pethidine

- This is an opiate-based drug given by injection.
- It quickly makes the mother feel relaxed because it causes the muscles to relax.
- This makes pain more tolerable, but it does not take the pain away altogether.
- Used in early labour, it can help the mother to settle and rest.
- Cannot be used too close to birth because the mother might not be sufficiently alert and it could make the baby sleepy. This could adversely affect feeding and even breathing.
- Pethidine can cause some mothers to feel sick or disoriented.

Epidural anaesthetic

- Local anaesthetic that numbs the nerves that carry the pain impulses from the birth canal to the brain.
- Can provide total pain relief, but not always 100 per cent effective.
- Often used when a mother is experiencing a very long or painful labour, or when a mother becomes distressed.
- Can only be given by an anaesthetist in hospital.
- The mother lies on her side or sits curled up. Local anaesthetic is used to numb the back then a needle is inserted. A tube passes through the needle into the back, near the nerves that carry pain impulses from the uterus. Drugs, usually a mixture of local anaesthetic and opioid, are administered through this tube.
- It takes about 10 minutes to administer an epidural, and up to another 15 minutes for it to work.
- It can then be topped up if necessary.
- An epidural does not usually cause sickness or drowsiness.
- Mother's contractions and the baby's heart rate will need to be continuously monitored.

Possible side effects include:

- legs feeling heavy
- blood pressure dropping (rare)
- prolonged second stage of labour as contractions may not be felt, leading to increased likelihood of assisted delivery
- difficulty passing urine
- a headache (this can be treated)
- a sore back for a day or two afterwards.

TENS

- TENS stands for 'transcutaneous electrical nerve stimulation'.
- A TENS machine is a small device that has leads connected to sticky pads called electrodes.
- These are attached to the mother's skin.
- Small electrical impulses are delivered – these give a tingling sensation.
- They reduce the pain signals going to the spinal cord and brain, relieving pain and relaxing muscles.
- It is possible that they also stimulate the production of endorphins – the body's 'natural painkillers'.
- For most people, TENS carries no side effects.

TENS should not be used:

- if the mother has a pacemaker or another type of electrical or metal implant
- if the mother has epilepsy or a heart problem
- in some cases, early in pregnancy.

www.hoddereducation.co.uk/myrevisionnotes

Water birth

- Water can help relaxation, and this makes contractions more bearable.
- Water should be kept at a comfortable temperature, not above 37.5°C.
- The mother's temperature will be monitored throughout. This is because a raised maternal temperature increases the oxygen requirement of the baby.

Figure 2.10 Waterbirth – water can help a mother to relax.

Breathing and relaxation techniques

See page 25.

Now test yourself

TESTED

1 Outline the three stages of labour.
2 Discuss **two** different birthing options
3 Discuss **three** methods of pain relief.

LO3: Understand postnatal checks, postnatal provision and conditions for development

3.1 The postnatal checks of the newborn baby REVISED

Straight after birth, the doctor/midwife carries out routine checks, checking for obvious physical problems.

Apgar score

- Evaluates the physical condition of a newborn, by assessing five vital signs:
  - heartbeat
  - breathing
  - muscle tone
  - reflex response (when the foot/nostril is stimulated)
  - colour.
- Reveals how well the baby is doing outside the mother's womb, and whether medical assistance is needed.
- This assessment is carried out one minute after birth, and again five minutes after birth.
- If there is a problem, reassessment may continue every five minutes.
- Scores are given out of ten (each sign can score between zero and two).
- Most healthy babies score nine – many of them lose a point because they have blue extremities, which can last for several hours.
- A paediatrician will be informed if there is a score of six or under after five minutes.
- Low scores at one minute are not so concerning, as many babies will score higher by five minutes.
- Babies who score between five and seven will be showing signs of mild asphyxia (lack of oxygen in the blood) and may need treatment.
- A score of between three and four indicates moderate asphyxia that will certainly need treatment.
- A baby scoring between zero and two has severe asphyxia and will need emergency resuscitation.

> **Apgar score** – score given to evaluate the physical condition of a newborn on assessment of their vital signs.

Skin

- A newborn's very thin skin is easily damaged.
- Skin takes about a month to mature into a protective barrier.
- Skin is checked for birthmarks.

Salmon patches (stork marks)

- Flat red/pink patches on eyelids, neck or forehead at birth.
- More noticeable when a baby cries as they fill with blood, becoming darker.
- Most fade completely in a few months.
- On the forehead or the back of neck, they can remain for four years or longer.

Mongolian spots

- Bluish patches of darker pigment, appearing mostly over the bottom and on black skin.
- Can be mistaken for bruises, but are harmless.
- Usually disappear by the age of four.

Infantile haemangiomas (strawberry marks)

- Raised marks, usually red.
- Appear anywhere on the body.
- Grow in the first six months, but then shrink and disappear, usually by seven years of age.

Vernix

- This is a white, waxy substance covering skin while in the womb.
- Apparent on newborns at birth.
- Natural moisturiser providing a protective layer that helps to prevent infection.
- Left to absorb naturally into the skin.
- In overdue babies, the vernix may have been absorbed while in the womb, leading to dry and cracked skin. This peels off on its own over a few days, revealing healthy skin underneath.

Lanugo

- At around 22 weeks of pregnancy, a baby begins to become covered in this soft, fine hair.
- It is usually unpigmented (without colour).
- Thought to help keep baby's body at the right temperature.
- Generally, shed during months 7–8 of pregnancy.
- Sometimes present in newborns, but disappears within days/weeks.

Physical checks

- Within 72 hours of birth, a thorough physical examination of the baby is offered.
- Continuing regular checks will monitor growth and development, enabling problems to be identified and treated early.

Weight

- Weight will be recorded in a Personal Child Health Record, given to all parents.
- Full-term babies usually weigh 2.7–4.1 kg.
- Weight is tracked on centile charts, which show the expected pattern of growth of a healthy baby, so that comparisons can be made.
- Steady weight gain indicates a baby that is healthy and feeding well.
- Babies tend to lose some of their birth weight within the first few days.
- This should soon be regained – usually within two weeks.
- Support will be given if this does not happen.

Length

- This is recorded on centile charts, so growth can be tracked.
- A full-term newborn's length is usually 50–53 cm.

Head circumference

- The shape of the head is assessed and the circumference measured.
- Used to track development over coming weeks/months.
- A squashed appearance is common, due to being squeezed through the birth canal.
- This usually resolves itself within two days.

Fontanelle

- Fontanelles are soft spots between the bones in the skull, where the skull bones have not yet fused together.
- There is one on the top of the head near the front, and a smaller one towards the back, covered by a tough protective membrane.
- Fontanelles will be checked – the bones won't join together for a year or more.

Eyes

- Tests do not reveal how well a baby can see.
- But they do check for cataracts and other conditions, through assessment of the appearance and movement of the eyes.
- A light is shone into the eyes to check a reflex.
- If a baby has cataracts, there will be a clouding of the transparent lens inside the eye.

Mouth

- A finger is placed in the mouth to check that the palate (roof of the mouth) is complete.
- The sucking reflex is also checked (see below).

> **Revision activity**
>
> Ask a parent if you can take a look at their child's centile charts. Study how they track development.

Feet

- Toes are counted and checked for webbing.
- The natural resting position of the feet and ankles will be observed to check for talipes (clubfoot) – a condition in which the front half of the foot turns in and down.

Fingers

- Fingers are counted and checked for webbing.
- Palms are checked to see if two creases (palmar creases), run across them.
- A single palmar crease is sometimes associated with Down's syndrome.

Hips

- A check is made for 'developmental dysplasia of the hip' – a condition in which the hip joints have not formed properly.
- This can result in joint problems or a limp if not identified and treated.

Reflexes

Newborns are observed to see if they display the expected reflexes. If these do not occur naturally, the baby's body may be stimulated to elicit the reflex medics wish to see.

- **Sucking reflex** – gently touch the roof of a baby's mouth and they will make sucking motions. This motion allows them to feed.
- **Rooting reflex** – when a baby's lips or cheek is touched, they move their head, searching for their mother's nipple/bottle teat to feed.
- **Grasp reflex** – if you touch a baby's palm, they will grasp your fingers with their fingers.
- **Standing and walking reflex** – when held upright with feet on a firm surface, newborns make stepping movements with their legs (but cannot take their weight).
- **Startle reflex** – if a baby wakes suddenly/hears a loud noise, they will make a fist with their hands and move stiff arms away from their body.

Figure 3.1 Reflexes

Now test yourself

TESTED

1 Discuss **five** checks carried out on a newborn baby.
2 Outline the different types of marks that may be visible on a baby's skin.
3 Discuss each type of reflex.

3.2 The specific needs of the pre-term (premature) baby

- Babies that need specific extra care when they are born will be cared for in a special care baby unit.
- Most commonly it is due to them being **pre-term** (premature).
- It is important that parents are still given time to bond with their baby.

> **Pre-term** – a baby born before week 37 of pregnancy (also called 'premature').

Birth before 37 weeks

- By around week 12 of pregnancy, a baby is formed.
- For the remaining weeks, they continue to develop and grow.
- Babies born before 37 weeks are not developed enough to survive outside the womb without medical help.

These babies are likely to have some or all of the following problems:

- breathing difficulties due to undeveloped lungs
- a weak immune system, making infection more likely
- inability to suck and swallow, difficulty digesting milk
- problems regulating body temperature
- low calcium/iron levels
- jaundice (yellow-tinged skin) or red wrinkled skin
- weak muscle tone and little movement
- sealed eyes
- low blood-sugar levels
- head that seems large in proportion to their body.

> **Exam tip**
>
> Think about how parents are likely to feel if their pre-term baby experiences some or all of the common problems. This will help you to understand the support needed at this time.

Pre-term babies

- Often need vitamins and mineral supplements for growth.
- Special formula milks are also available, although it is best to breastfeed.
- If too weak to feed normally, babies will be fed through a tube into a vein – an intravenous (IV) line.
- Or they may be fed through a fine tube that goes into the stomach – via the nose/throat/through the mouth.

Specific needs

Treatment for infection

- Some babies acquire an infection during the birth.
- There is also a risk of acquiring an infection after the birth.
- In addition to having an immature immune system, the specific care experiences and interventions needed by pre-term babies make them vulnerable to infection.

Treatments may be given for:

- bacterial infections – antibiotics
- fungal infections – anti-fungal medications
- viral infections – supportive measures, such as good nutrition (specific treatments exist for some viruses).

Breathing problems

- Unborn babies' lungs are filled with liquid that helps them develop.
- During labour and birth this is absorbed, so that air can be taken in once born.
- In pre-term babies, the lungs are often not mature enough to adjust after birth.
- Healthcare professionals will provide help that is as gentle as possible, because ventilators (a machine that helps with breathing) can cause lung problems.

Feeding problems

- If a gap in the roof of the mouth is picked up during the mouth check, the baby has a 'cleft palate'.
- This makes feeding difficult, and surgery is necessary.
- If a baby has persistent problems latching on during breastfeeding, they are checked for 'tongue-tie'.
  - This is when tongue movement is restricted because the tongue is anchored to the bottom of the mouth by a piece of skin that is too short and tight.
  - A simple procedure generally overcomes this immediately.
- It is common for parents to experience feeding issues, and they may need information, advice and support.

> **Common mistake**
>
> Remember that specific needs are not always due to a baby being born prematurely. Take care not to imply this in the answers you give.

Figure 3.2 Parents need time to bond with their new baby.

Now test yourself

TESTED

1 Explain when a baby is considered to be pre-term.
2 Discuss why a pre-term baby is at increased risk of infection.
3 Discuss **one** possible cause of feeding problems.

3.3 The postnatal provision available for the mother and baby and the postnatal needs of the family

- The support needed depends on the individual baby and family.
- However, postnatal provision is very important for the well-being of all concerned.
- Parents may need support as they adjust their lifestyles.
- There will also be an impact on close family members, such as siblings.

The role of the father/partner

The father/partner:

- has a very significant role
- needs time to bond with the new baby alongside the mother
- may be best placed to help and support the mother through difficult early days/weeks of motherhood – taking care of a new baby takes a great deal of time and energy
- can support the mother to take the time to take care of herself too, to stay fit and healthy, and to recover from the birth.

Support from other family and friends

- This can be a huge help to new parents.
- Of particular help if their relationship comes under pressure as they adjust to new responsibilities.
- Practical help and advice is valuable (for example, helping with shopping, sharing childcare tips).
- Some new parents need a lot of support from those more experienced in childcare.

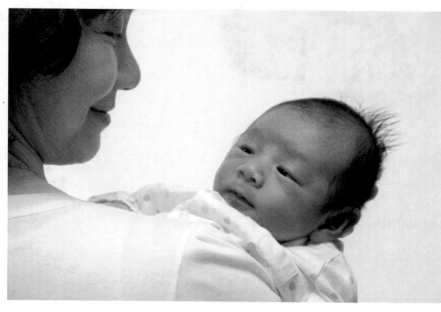

Figure 3.3 Some new parents need a lot of support from those more experienced in childcare.

> **Revision activity**
>
> Ask parents to tell you about the support they received from their family and close friends in the early weeks of parenthood. What difference did this make to them?

Information, advice and support from the GP, midwife and health visitor

- Health visitors give families support from pregnancy until children are five.
- They ensure children are healthy and developing normally.
- When a child is ill, the GP is usually the first point of contact.
- GPs liaise with others, including health visitors.
- This is to ensure that families get necessary treatment, information and advice.

Postnatal check 6 weeks after birth

- These checks ensure that the mother feels well and she is recovering from the birth.
- Not offered in every area, but mothers can request an appointment for a check, especially if there are concerns.
- No set guidelines for what should be covered in the check.

6–8-week review by a health visitor or doctor

- In this review, the baby's newborn physical examination is repeated. A mother can also expect:
  - questions about how she is feeling (to check on her mental health and well-being)
  - questions about vaginal discharge and whether there has been a period since the birth
  - a blood pressure check
  - an examination to see if stitches have healed (if relevant)
  - to be asked about contraception
  - to be weighed if overweight/obese, and to receive weight loss advice, healthy eating and physical activity guidance.
- Parents can contact their midwife, health visitor or GP to ask for help/advice.
- They can drop in to local clinics to speak to somebody from the health visiting team.

> **Common mistake**
>
> Do not fall into the trap of implying that reviews and routine visits will meet every healthcare need. For urgent queries that involve the health of a baby, parents should contact their GP, NHS 111 or go to an NHS walk-in centre/ nearest A&E department as soon as possible.

Now test yourself

TESTED ☐

1 Discuss the postnatal provision available for mother and baby.
2 Outline **five** ways in which the father/partner can support the mother.
3 Discuss the support that may be needed from family and close friends.

3.4 Conditions for development

In order for them to successfully thrive, develop and grow, children need certain basic conditions, as shown in Figure 3.4.

The importance of the environment to the child

A positive environment is crucial to a child, and the following needs must be met.

Love and security

All children need to feel:

- loved
- wanted
- nurtured.

This gives rise to feeling emotionally secure. Children also need to be kept:

- physically secure
- safe from harm (see page 48).

Warmth

To keep children warm they need sufficient:

- heating in the home
- clothing
- bedding.

Rest/sleep

- These are crucial for a child's physical health and well-being, learning, growth and development.
- The amount a child requires is often underestimated.

Exercise/fresh air

- These are good for a child's physical health and well-being.
- Young children are built to be busy and active.

Sufficient exercise:

- builds fitness
- builds robustness
- helps strong growth and development.

A lack of exercise can have a very negative effect on:

- health
- fitness
- development.

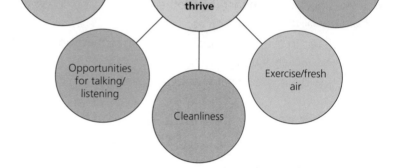

Figure 3.4 **To successfully thrive, develop and grow, children need certain basic conditions.**

Cleanliness

- Children need clean and appropriately hygienic environments.
- As their immune systems are less mature, it is much easier for a child to pick up an infection.
- Cleanliness in kitchen areas is especially important.
- The child must also be bathed daily and kept clean and fresh.
- Their clothing and bedding should be regularly laundered.

Stimulation/opportunities to play

- All children need opportunities to play in ways that are appropriate to their stage of development.
- Under the UN Convention on the Rights of the Child, all children have a fundamental right to play.

Opportunities for listening and talking

- Listening and talking with a child shows that you care about them and are interested in them.
- This is very important to their social and emotional development.
- It is also vital for their intellectual and language development – just think of all the things a child learns in conversation.

Routine (for example bedtime, bathtime, feeding)

Routines help young children to feel safe and secure. They also help adults to ensure that all of the child's care needs can be met effectively every day – for instance, feeding needs to be spread out across the day to ensure that children have the nutrition they need to keep them going. The bedtime routine can help a child to settle down and feel ready for sleep. For instance, many parents choose to bath their children in the evening, then put them to bed and read them a story, before leaving them to sleep.

Awareness of Sudden Infant Death Syndrome (SIDS)

Parents and carers should know how to take measures to prevent SIDS.

Common mistake

It is easy to fall into the trap of focussing solely on talking with children, because on the surface, this seems like the most active part of communicating with them. However, listening to children is equally important, and crucial to children's emotional well-being, as well as their learning.

Figure 3.5 Listening and talking with a child shows that you care about them.

Figure 3.6 Stories are often part of the bedtime routine.

Revision activity

1. Visit this NHS weblink and read more about SIDS: www.nhs.uk/Conditions/Sudden-infant-death-syndrome/Pages/Introduction.aspx
2. Follow at least two of the weblinks given on the NHS web page and read the information you come across.
3. Make notes on the key points.

The need for acceptable patterns of behaviour and approaches to discipline

- Children need to learn how to behave in socially acceptable ways.
- Adults should always strive to be positive role models for children.
- A consistent approach to discipline is also needed, or a child may become confused, unsure or even worried about the reaction their behaviour will elicit.

Need for boundaries

- Children need to be aware of the boundaries set for their behaviour (they need to know what they are and are not allowed do).
- Boundaries should be consistent – it is unfair to send a child mixed messages.
- By always explaining why a particular behaviour is unacceptable, you can help a child to think through a situation.
- Then they will begin to moderate their own behaviour in similar situations in future.

Consideration of others

- If you ask a parent what behaviour trait they would like to see in their child, they will often say that they want them to be kind and considerate towards other people.
- We value this highly in our society.
- Young children need a lot of support when they are learning how to be considerate, because it is natural for them to notice and act upon their own feelings ahead of someone else's.
- For instance, they might snatch a toy away from a peer because their desire for the item is greater than their awareness of how this could upset another child.
- In time and with lots of role modelling and talking through social situations, children are increasingly able to be considerate in more situations.
- Toddlers can be seen being very empathetic with another child who has hurt themselves, for instance.

Safety

- A lot of the rules we make are in place because they keep children safe – from holding hands when crossing the road to not being allowed to stand on the table.
- It is important that these rules are explained so that children gradually become more aware of how to keep themselves safe independently.

Promoting positive behaviour

- Promoting positive behaviour is by far the best way to limit inappropriate behaviour.
- When adults notice and praise specific positive behaviour, a child tends to feel proud of themselves, and they enjoy the approval they receive.
- This encourages them to repeat the socially acceptable behaviour, until it becomes an ingrained, normal part of what they do.
- Verbal praise is the most effective form of praise, and the easiest to give.
- If there is a behaviour goal in place for a child, a reward chart can also be an effective visual reward system.

Figure 3.7 **Toddlers can be empathetic towards one another.**

Now test yourself

TESTED ☐

1 Discuss the basic conditions children need to successfully thrive, develop and grow.
2 Explain the measures parents and carers should know to take to prevent SIDS.
3 Discuss how to promote positive behaviour.

LO4: Understand how to recognise, manage and prevent childhood illnesses

4.1 How immunity to disease and infection can be acquired

REVISED

Babies' natural immunity

- During pregnancy, **antibodies** from the mother are passed to an unborn baby through the placenta.
- Some **immunity** can also be passed on through breastfeeding.
- The mother can only pass on immunity that she has herself (so if a mother hasn't had chickenpox, she will not have developed immunity against it, so no chickenpox antibodies will be passed on).
- Childhood immunisations begin at two months old, because any immunity received from the mother is temporary.
- Babies receive antibodies in the last three months of pregnancy.
- So, the immune system of premature babies is not as strong because they have had fewer antibodies passed to them. This puts them at a higher risk of disease.

Childhood immunisations and vaccination programmes

- **Vaccination** helps to protect children against a range of serious and potentially fatal diseases.
- To protect children in the UK, the NHS offers a free programme of immunisations to every child. This is known as the 'routine immunisation schedule' (see Table 4.1).

Reasons for immunisation

The NHS says there are three good reasons to have a child vaccinated:

- Vaccinations are quick, safe and extremely effective.
- Once a child has been vaccinated against a disease, their body can more successfully fight it off.
- If a child is not vaccinated, they are at higher risk of catching and becoming very ill from the illness.

There will always be some children who are unavoidably unprotected because:

- they can't be vaccinated for medical reasons
- they are too young to be vaccinated
- they can't get to the vaccine clinics
- the vaccine doesn't work (although this is rare).

However, if more parents have their children vaccinated, then a greater number of children in the community will be protected against an illness.

> **Immunity** – when an organism has the ability to resist disease.
>
> **Antibodies** – proteins made by the body that can latch on to foreign viruses and bacteria, making them ineffective.
>
> **Vaccine/vaccination** – a biological preparation that provides or improves immunity to a specific disease, commonly given via an injection.

> **Exam tip**
>
> Ensure that you are clear about the definition of key words **immunity, antibodies** and **vaccine/vaccination**. Take care to use these words correctly in the answers that you give.

Table 4.1 Excerpt from the NHS routine immunisation schedule

Age due	Diseases protected against	Vaccine given	Trade name	Usual site
Eight weeks	Diphtheria, tetanus, pertussis (whooping cough), polio, *Haemophilus influenzae* type b (Hib)	DTaP/IPV/Hib	Pediacel or Infanrix IPV Hib	Thigh
	Pneumococcal (13 serotypes)	Pneumococcal conjugate vaccine (PCV)	Prevenar 13	Thigh
	Meningococcal group B (MenB)	MenB	Bexsero	Left thigh
	Rotavirus gastroenteritis	Rotavirus	Rotarix	By mouth
Twelve weeks	Diphtheria, tetanus, pertussis, polio, Hib	DTaP/IPV/Hib	Pediacel or Infanrix IPV Hib	Thigh
	Meningococcal group C (MenC)	MenC	NeisVac-C	Thigh
	Rotavirus	Rotavirus	Rotarix	By mouth
Sixteen weeks	Diphtheria, tetanus, pertussis, polio, Hib	DTaP/IPV/Hib	Pediacel or Infanrix IPV Hib	Thigh
	MenB	MenB	Bexsero	Left thigh
	Pneumococcal (13 serotypes)	PCV	Prevenar 13	Thigh
One year old	Hib and MenC	Hib/MenC booster	Menitorix	Upper arm/thigh
	Pneumococcal (13 serotypes)	PCV booster	Prevenar 13	Upper arm/thigh
	Measles, mumps and rubella (German measles)	MMR	MMR VaxPRO or Priorix	Upper arm/thigh
	MenB	MenB booster	Bexsero	Left thigh
Two to six years old (including children in school years 1 and 2)	Influenza (each year from September)	Live attenuated influenza vaccine LAIV3	Fluenz Tetra	Both nostrils
Three years four months old	Diphtheria, tetanus, pertussis and polio	DTaP/IPV	Infanrix IPV or Repevax	Upper arm
	Measles, mumps and rubella	MMR (check first dose given)	MMR VaxPRO or Priorix	Upper arm

- **Additional** vaccines may be offered to children with underlying medical conditions – for example, severe asthma, heart failure or diabetes.
- **Selective** vaccines may be offered to children with a higher risk of hepatitis B or tuberculosis.

Revision activity

Visit this website to browse NHS information about vaccinations: https://tinyurl.com/qzx5fsd

Figure 4.1 Vaccinations are quick, safe and extremely effective.

Now test yourself

TESTED

1 Explain why babies have natural immunity at birth.
2 Outline the free programme of childhood immunisations offered by the NHS in the UK.
3 Discuss why there will always be some children who are unavoidably unprotected against diseases for which childhood vaccinations exist.

4.2 How to recognise and treat common childhood ailments and diseases

REVISED

To successfully recognise and treat common childhood ailments and diseases, you need to know about:

- general signs of illness
- common childhood ailments and diseases
- caring for a sick child
- when to seek treatment by a doctor
- when to seek emergency medical help.

General signs of illness

Children who become ill in your care may display the following signs and symptoms of illness:

- vomiting and diarrhoea
- high temperature
- tiredness/disturbed sleep
- reduced appetite
- flushed or pale complexion/lip area
- irritable/fretful behaviour
- lack of desire to play
- headache
- swollen glands
- runny/blocked-up nose
- cough.

You should also be aware that:

- You will often see two or more of these signs together.
- For instance, a child coming down with a cold may have a blocked-up nose, a cough and a reduced appetite.

A child displaying any of these symptoms will need monitoring and sympathetic care (see 'Caring for an ill child' on page 54). Signs of specific ailments and diseases are given in Table 4.2.

Figure 4.2 A child coming down with a cold may have a blocked-up nose, a cough and a reduced appetite.

Common childhood ailments and diseases

Carefully read the information in Table 4.2.

Caring for an ill child

In the next section, you will revise emergency situations in which you will need to act calmly and quickly to help an ill child. (Also see 'Food intolerances and allergies' on page 58, and 'The needs of an ill child' on page 62.)

Now test yourself

TESTED

1 Outline **five** general signs of illness.
2 Explain the signs and symptoms of the common cold.
3 Discuss the treatment for tonsillitis.

Revision activity

Think about the last time you were too unwell to go to school. Write down how you felt, and how you wanted people to treat you. This will help you to understand the sympathetic care needed by an ill child.

Table 4.2 Childhood ailments and diseases.

Ailment/ disease	Spread	Signs and symptoms	Rash or specific sign	Treatment
Common cold	Airborne/droplet, hand-to-hand contact Incubation 1–3 days	Sore throat, sneezing running nose, headache, slight fever, irritability, partial deafness		Treat symptoms
Chickenpox	Airborne/droplet, direct contact Incubation 10–14 days	Slight fever, itchy rash, mild onset then child feels ill, often with a severe headache	Red spots with a white centre on trunk and limbs at first; blisters and pustules	Rest, fluids, calamine on rash, cut child's nails to prevent secondary infection
Food poisoning	Indirect: infected food or drink Incubation 30 minutes–36 hours	Vomiting, diarrhoea, abdominal pain		Fluids only for 24 hours; medical aid if no better or in babies
Gastroenteritis	Direct contact Incubation 7–14 days Indirect: infected food or drink Incubation 30 minutes–36 hours	Vomiting, diarrhoea, signs of dehydration		Replace fluids – water (or Dioralyte) Medical aid is needed urgently
Measles	Airborne/droplet Incubation 7–15 days	High fever, fretful, heavy cold – running nose and discharge from eyes. Later a cough	Day 1: Koplik's spots (clustered white lesions inside mouth) Day 4: blotchy rash begins to spread on face and body	Rest, fluids, tepid sponging, shaded room if light is uncomfortable to eyes
Mumps	Airborne/droplet Incubation 14–21 days	Pain, swelling of jaw in front of ears, fever, eating and drinking painful	Swollen face	Fluids given via a straw (if child is old enough to manage this), hot compresses, oral hygiene
Pertussis (whooping cough)	Airborne/droplet, direct contact Incubation 7–21 days	Starts with a snuffly cold, slight cough, mild fever	Spasmodic cough with whoop sound, vomiting	Rest and reassurance, feed after coughing attack, support during attack, steam inhalations as advised by a doctor
Rubella (German measles)	Airborne/droplet Incubation 7–14 days	Slight cold, sore throat, mild fever, swollen glands behind ears, pain in small joints	Slight pink rash starts behind ears and on forehead – not itchy	Rest if necessary Treat symptoms
Scarlet fever	Droplet Incubation 2–4 days	Sudden fever, loss of appetite, sore throat, pallor around mouth	Bright red pinpoint rash over face and body – may peel	Rest, fluids and observe for complications, antibiotics
Tonsillitis	Direct infection, droplet	Very sore throat, fever, headache, pain on swallowing, aches and pains in back and limbs		Rest, fluids, medical aid, antibiotics Iced drinks to relieve pain

4.3 When to seek treatment and help – the key signs and symptoms

REVISED

When to seek treatment by a doctor

You revised the general signs of illness in the last section. Children displaying these signs may need treatment from a doctor if the signs worsen, persist, or if there are complications.

- You should always be cautious with children's health.
- If you are worried, it is far better to call the doctor or the NHS advice line 111 for advice than to delay.

When to seek emergency medical help

The following signs and symptoms of illness indicate that you need to call for urgent medical attention – i.e. that you need to call an ambulance:

- breathing difficulties
- convulsions/seizures/fitting
- child seems to be in significant pain
- child is unresponsive – cannot easily or fully be roused from sleep, or a state of drowsiness
- baby becomes unresponsive and/or their body seems to be floppy or limp
- severe headache which may be accompanied by a stiff neck or a dislike of light
- rash that remains (does not fade) when pressed with a glass
- vomiting that persists for over 24 hours
- unusual, high-pitched crying in babies
- high fever/temperature that cannot be lowered
- will not drink fluids – this is most worrying in babies.

Common mistake

Students sometimes confuse when to call the doctor or the NHS advice line 111, and when to call an ambulance. When you are advised to call for 'urgent medical attention', this means that it is an emergency and you need to call an ambulance without delay.

Meningitis

A child with meningitis may have the following symptoms:

- a high temperature or fever
- vomiting
- severe headache
- stiff neck
- drowsiness
- confusion
- dislike of bright lights
- seizures (fitting)
- a skin rash of red/purple 'pinprick' spots
  - if these spots spread they can resemble fresh bruising (this is hard to see on black skin)
  - the rash will not fade when the side of a glass is pressed against it.

In babies, there may also be restlessness and a high-pitched crying or screaming, as well as:

- a limp or floppy body
- swelling of the fontanelle area of the skull (the soft spot on the top of the head)
- refusal to feed.

A doctor must be called immediately, because meningitis can be life-threatening, and the child might deteriorate quickly.

- If they cannot be contacted or are delayed, call 999 (or 112 from a mobile) for an ambulance.
- Do not wait for all of the symptoms to appear.
- If a casualty has already seen a doctor but is becoming worse, seek urgent medical attention again – call for an ambulance.
- Reassure the casualty and keep them cool until help arrives.

> **Revision activity**
>
> Download this free app that will tell you all you need to know about meningitis.
>
> It has saved lives, because people can check the symptoms instantly if they are concerned about a child: www.meningitisnow.org/meningitis-explained/signs-and-symptoms/download-our-mobile-app/

Asthma

- When an asthma attack occurs, the airways go into spasm, making breathing difficult.
- This may occur after contact with allergens such as dust, pollen or pet hair.
- It can also be caused by the child having a cold, experiencing stress or extreme cold.
- The severity of attacks varies, but they can be serious and life-threatening.
- They can also be very frightening.
- The casualty may cough, wheeze and become breathless.

If a child is known to be asthmatic, they should have a 'reliever' inhaler immediately available.

- These are generally blue, and deliver medication to the lungs to relieve affected airways.
- Reassure and give the inhaler as instructed.
- Children and young people may also have another type of inhaler used to prevent attacks.
- Make sure you know which to use in an emergency.
- Sit the casualty upright and leaning forwards in a comfortable position – they should never lie down.
- Stay with them.
- If this is the first attack or the condition persists or worsens, call for an ambulance.

Figure 4.3 A 'reliever' inhaler delivers medication to the lungs.

Seizures (fitting)

- May be due to epilepsy or a high temperature.
- There may be violent muscle twitching, clenched fists and an arched back, which may lead to unconsciousness.
- An ambulance should be called.
- Instead of trying to restrain the casualty, the immediate area should be cleared and the casualty should be surrounded with pillows or padding for protection.
- The casualty should be cooled gradually (as for a temperature, see below).
- If the seizure stops before help arrives, the casualty can be placed in the recovery position (see page 76).

High temperatures

- The normal temperature reading for a child is between 36.5°C and 37.4°C.
- Children may have a higher temperature when they are ill.
- Taking a child's temperature with a digital or feverscan thermometer helps you to monitor their illness (these come with directions for use).

You should take steps to lower a temperature by:

- ensuring that warm clothing is removed so that just a cool layer is worn
- providing a cool drink, either water or another drink diluted with water.

Some children may be given paracetamol syrup by parents or carers (for example, if a child is prone to convulsions brought on by a high temperature).

Common mistake

Children may also have a high or higher temperature after physical activity or having hot food or hot drinks. You should therefore avoid taking their temperature at these times.

Now test yourself

TESTED ☐

1 Explain when emergency treatment should be sought for a child.
2 Outline how to bring down a high temperature.
3 Discuss what to do if you identify signs of meningitis.
4 Explain how you would recognise and treat an asthma attack.

4.4 Diet-related illnesses

Some children experience illnesses that are related to diet.

Childhood obesity

- Children can be at risk of becoming obese with incorrect nutrition.
- The NHS tells us that very overweight children tend to grow up to be very overweight adults
- This can lead to serious health problems.

Children who are of a healthy weight tend to be fitter, healthier, better able to learn and more self-confident.

The NHS recommends five key ways to help children achieve a healthy weight:

- encouraging 60 minutes of physically active play each day – for young children this will occur in several short bursts throughout the day
- providing healthy meals, drinks and snacks
- keeping to child-size portions
- sufficient sleep
- being a good role model (for example, eating healthily and being physically active).

Deficiency diseases

- Children can be at risk of developing deficiency diseases if they do not receive the necessary nutrition.
- This includes vitamins and minerals.
- You can read more about this in the textbook, on pages 112 and 113 of Unit R019.

Food intolerances and allergies

- Some children have food allergies, intolerances or medical conditions that mean their diets have to be restricted.
- Such conditions include diabetes or an enzyme deficiency.

It is very important to ensure that you fully understand children's dietary requirements so that you can meet their needs without error.

Key facts:

- In a setting, practitioners should ensure that full details of diet restrictions are recorded on a child's registration form.
- They must also communicate the child's requirements to everyone involved in caring for them.
- A list of the child's requirements should be displayed in the kitchen and eating area to remind all staff.
- You must never give a child food or drink without checking that it is safe for them to have.
- This also applies to raw cooking ingredients or food used in play that is not intended for consumption.
- Common allergens include nuts and cows' milk.
- Some children (for example those with diabetes) may need to eat at certain times of the day.
- Children might take medication daily.

Children might have medication to take if they show symptoms of their condition or if you become aware that they have eaten – or in the case of some children, even touched – a food they should not have.

● Often, time is of the essence in these situations.

● You must ensure that you are absolutely clear about what to do for an individual child, and you must know how to recognise their symptoms.

● **This could save a life.**

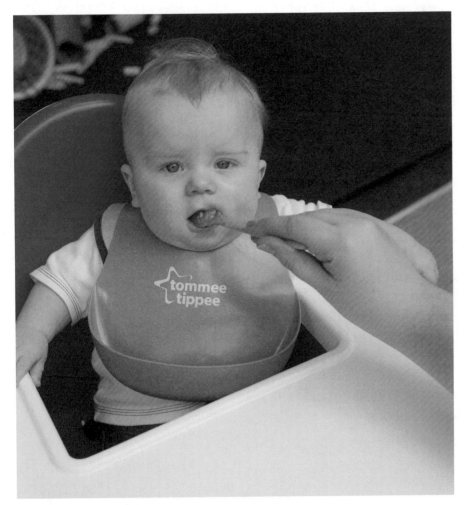

Figure 4.4 Never give a child food or drink without checking that it is safe for them to have

Anaphylactic shock

● **Anaphylactic shock** is a severe allergic reaction and a life-threatening situation.

● An ambulance must be called immediately.

Anaphylactic shock can be caused by any allergens, but common triggers include nuts, eggs and shellfish.

Signs of anaphylactic shock:

● red, itchy rash or blotchy skin that becomes raised

● swelling of face, hands, feet

● pale or flushed skin

● puffy/red/itchy/watery eyes

● wheezing/difficulty breathing

> **Anaphylactic shock** – a severe allergic reaction, and a life-threatening situation.

- swelling of tongue and throat
- abdominal pain
- vomiting/diarrhoea
- agitation/confusion
- signs of shock.

To treat anaphylactic shock, a first aider will:

- call for an ambulance
- check if the casualty has their own auto-injector of adrenaline and if so, administer (if trained to do so)
- help the child to sit in a position that aids breathing
- monitor and assess until help arrives
- if the casualty becomes pale with a weak pulse, treat for shock – lie them down and raise their legs.

Diabetes

- In children with diabetes, the body doesn't produce the hormone insulin.
- This in turn affects the body's ability to process the sugar or glucose found in food.
- To counteract this, most children with diabetes will need to have insulin injections at various times of the day.
- If they have either too much or too little insulin in their body, a child can experience the following serious conditions:
  - hypoglycaemia (often called a 'hypo') – the blood sugar level is too low
  - hyperglycaemia (often called a 'hyper') – the blood sugar level is too high.

Hypoglycaemia

Signs and symptoms of a hypoglycaemic attack (hypo) include:

- drowsiness with a deteriorating level of response
- feeling weak or faint
- feeling hungry
- confusion or irritability/behaving irrationally
- palpitations
- muscle tremors (trembling)
- sweating and cold, clammy, pale skin
- rapid pulse.

Managing a hypo

- A hypo is often caused by more exercise than usual or lack of food at the right time.
- The casualty needs to get sugar into their system to balance out the insulin level, which is incorrect.
- Children with diabetes will have a care plan, and practitioners will know what to give them if they show signs of a hypo.
  - This might be a sugary drink such as orange juice, chocolate or a tube of special glucose gel.
  - The child will bring this to the setting with them.

If impaired consciousness has already occurred, the attack is in an advanced stage and an ambulance is needed. If at an earlier stage, a first aider will:

- sit the child down
- give them their drink/gel as described above
- if they respond, give them more food and drink until they feel better
- encourage the child to rest; they may have the equipment with them (a glucose testing kit) to check their own glucose levels.

If the child doesn't respond an ambulance is needed.

- The first aider will monitor and record the level of response, breathing and pulse, and also remain alert to other reasons for the symptoms.

Hyperglycaemia

Signs and symptoms of a hyperglycaemic attack (hyper) include:

- drowsiness, resulting in impaired consciousness/unconsciousness if not treated
- feeling very thirsty
- rapid breathing
- warm, dry skin
- rapid pulse
- fruity, sweet-smelling breath
- passing urine frequently.

Managing a hyper

- A hyper develops slowly over a few days.
- It requires emergency medical treatment to prevent the casualty from falling into a diabetic coma (unconsciousness brought on by diabetes).

A first aider will:

- call for an ambulance
- monitor and record the level of response, breathing and pulse.

If a casualty loses consciousness, the first aider will open the airway, check breathing and be ready to start CPR if necessary.

Now test yourself

TESTED ☐

1 Discuss the implications of caring for a child who has an allergy or food intolerance.
2 Outline **six** signs of anaphylactic shock.
3 Outline ways of helping children to maintain a healthy weight.
4 Explain how you would recognise a hypoglycaemic attack (hypo).

4.5 The needs of an ill child

When a child is unwell, they rely on adults to meet all of their needs. These fall into four categories, as shown in Figure 4.5.

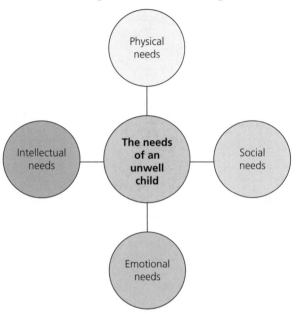

Figure 4.5 The needs of an unwell child

Physical needs

- When a child is sick, they need plenty of rest.
  - o Usual routines often need to be adjusted to allow for extra naps, particularly if night-time sleep has been disturbed (for example through coughing or vomiting).
- Children's diets may need to be adjusted – if they have an upset stomach for example.
- It is always important to ensure that plenty of water (or diluted juice) is taken.
- You should always monitor a sick child carefully, as conditions can worsen suddenly.
- You should be ready to call for medical help if necessary.
- You should also make sure that you are aware of a child's medical conditions (such as asthma or diabetes) and that you know what to do should there be a problem.
- High temperatures or fevers are often seen in young children, so you should know how to care for a child experiencing these (see page 57).

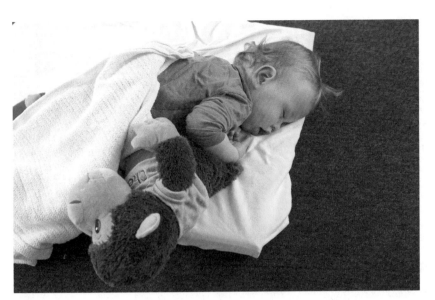

Figure 4.6 If a child is feeling unwell, they need plenty of rest.

Social and emotional needs

It can be confusing and frightening for a child to suddenly feel unwell.

- An ill child needs empathy and plenty of reassurance, especially when they are too young to understand how they feel.
- Adults should gently explain the illness to a child, and if appropriate, let them know that they will feel better soon.
- Talking positively about any medication, naps and healthy eating can also help.
- Children's desire to have company may be just as strong as ever, so activities you can do together are especially helpful.
- Children might need extra physical affection, such as cuddles or sitting on your lap.

Also bear in mind that an ill child may also regress in their behaviour, going back temporarily to things they did that brought them comfort when they were younger (examples include clinging to an adult's legs or sucking their thumb).

Intellectual needs

- Children are likely to need quiet activities to keep them amused and stimulated while they are not up to more active play.
- Stories, colouring activities and IT devices are popular choices.
- If a child is ill or will be recovering for a longer period, it is important to think carefully about activities that will help their learning and development to continue as expected.
- If appropriate, visits from friends and family will also be beneficial, as children can miss wider social contact.

> **Revision activity**
>
> Spend some time talking to a parent of a young child. Ask them to explain to you how the care needs of their child changed during his or her last period of illness. What did the parent need to do differently to ensure that these care needs were met?

Now test yourself

TESTED

1. Discuss ways in which you may need to adjust the routine of an unwell young child, in order to meet their physical needs.
2. Suggest **two** ways in which an unwell child may regress in their behaviour.
3. Outline **three** quiet activities you could provide to help keep an unwell child amused and stimulated while they are not up to more active play.

4.6 How to prepare a child for a stay in hospital

REVISED

Going into hospital can be a worrying time for anyone – especially for young children.

- Sometimes hospital admission happens very quickly in an emergency.
- When admission is planned, adults have time to prepare the child.
  - This can make a big difference to the levels of anxiety felt by both a child and their family.

Hospital/ward visit

- Adults, as well as children, often worry about the unknown – not knowing enough about a place or a situation in advance can make you nervous.
- Therefore, a hospital visit can lead you to imagine scary scenarios.
- This is no different for children – so if a child has not been to hospital before, or they have not stayed on a particular ward before, it is a good idea to arrange a visit with hospital staff.
  - Being able to see where their bed will be, where their toys will be and meeting friendly staff can really put children at ease.
  - If parents will be staying at the hospital, it will help for the child to see where they will sleep.

Figure 4.7 **You should prepare a child for a hospital stay.**

Acting out fears and hospital games

- Imaginary play is a wonderful, safe way for children to act out and explore their fears.
- This helps them to prepare for real-life situations, and gives them reassurance.
- Hospital games can be played with just a few resources, such as a toy doctor's kit with a play stethoscope, thermometer, syringe, etc. Teddies or dolls make perfect patients.
- In group settings, hospital uniforms are popular additions to the dressing up clothes.

Books and DVDs

- There are many story books, non-fiction books, DVDs and even children's TV programmes that explore going into hospital.
- These have been written especially to help children become familiar with the environment before they have their own experience.
- The characters featured can also become strong role models for a child.

Explanation and honesty

- During a hospital stay, and when preparing for the stay at home, it is very important to explain what will happen in simple terms.
- You should always be gentle but honest. This includes answering children's questions honestly.
- It can be tempting not to admit that procedures might leave children feeling uncomfortable or sore.
- If a child learns that they cannot trust you, they will feel considerably more anxious in the long term, and might no longer be reassured by the things you say, even when they are true.
- However, it is important to stress the benefits of going into hospital, and the positive impact that any procedures will have for the child.

Involvement in a child's care

- Parents and carers are often able to be quite involved in their child's care while they are in hospital.
- In some circumstances, they may even be able to sleep on the ward or in the building.
- Parents can often continue with many aspects of the child's care, such as feeding, bathing and changing nappies.
- This continuity of care can help young children to feel more settled, secure and relaxed.

> **Revision activity**
>
> Visit this NHS website: www.nhs.uk/conditions/pregnancy-and-baby/pages/going-to-hospital.aspx and watch the video clip.

Now test yourself

TESTED ☐

1 Discuss **three** ways in which you would prepare a child for a stay in hospital.
2 Discuss why it is important to give a child who will be going into hospital the opportunity to act out their fears through play.
3 Explain **two** ways in which parents might be able to be involved in the care of a child in hospital.

Learning Outcome 5: Know about child safety

5.1 How to create a safe, child-friendly environment

REVISED

- Adults should make a child's environment as safe as possible.
- This means carrying out a risk assessment.
- A practitioner thinks carefully about a particular space, and identifies all of the apparent **hazards**.
- They then take steps to reduce the **risk** of the hazard causing harm to an acceptable level.
- There will always be accidents; we cannot wrap children up in cotton wool.
- But we can do our best to protect children from foreseeable accidents.

> **Hazard** – an item or situation that may cause harm.
>
> **Risk** – the likelihood of a hazard actually causing harm.

A hazard is an item or situation that could cause harm to a child, and potential hazards are all around us. They include:

- physical hazards – unsafe objects, things that may be tripped over, etc.
- security hazards – insecure exits and windows, etc.
- fire hazards – heaters, electrical appliances, etc.
- food safety hazards – faulty refrigerator, unsafe produce, etc.
- personal safety hazards – stranger danger, busy roads, etc.

Within the home

- Most accidents occur at home.
- Consider child development when risk assessing – for example a 12-month-old is likely to pull themselves up on a chair, which might be unsafe, or to open low kitchen cupboards when sitting on the floor.
- Children's awareness of danger also varies at different ages.

Hazards likely to be found in specific rooms are listed below.

Kitchen

- unsafe chemicals children could handle
- food safety hazards
- dangerously hot equipment
- sharp equipment
- fragile items that become dangerous when broken
- electronic food preparation equipment
- access to power sockets
- access to hot taps
- access to water (drowning risk)
- window from which a child could fall.

Bathroom

- unsafe chemicals for children to handle
- sharp equipment
- access to hot taps and hot water
- access to water (drowning risk)
- access to items unhygienic for children to handle – toilet brush, etc.
- access to items that are slippery when wet
- window from which a child could fall.

Living room

- access to electrical items and their power cords
- computers, phones
- access to power sockets
- access to heating source
- access to furniture that could tip, be climbed on or pulled over
- access to glass doors
- access to ornaments
- window from which a child could fall.

Bedroom

- access to power sockets
- access to heating source
- access to TV, DVD player
- access to electric blanket, hot water bottle
- access to furniture that could tip, be climbed on or pulled over
- window from which a child could fall.

Stairs

- items left on the stairs that could be tripped over
- risk of tripping
- risk of falling
- faulty or missing handrail.

Garden/play areas

Specific things to consider when children play in a garden or outside play areas, include:

- Are gates, sheds and any boundary fences secure?
- Can strangers or animals come into contact with children?
- Are there any problems caused by weather (icy patches, waterlogged areas, etc.)?
- Is there shelter from the sun/will children need sun protection?
- Are there any other risks from water (ponds, water courses, gullies, etc.)?
- Are litter bins and drains secure?
- Is the area free of litter, glass, poisonous plants and animal faeces?
- Have any items/equipment that could cause harm been left out?
- Is play equipment assembled safely? Is it age appropriate?
- Is safety flooring in good condition? Are mats needed under play equipment?

Figure 5.1 Play equipment must be age appropriate.

Revision activity

Imagine that you will be looking after a toddler in your home for an afternoon. You plan to make some cakes together. Go into your kitchen and conduct a risk assessment.

Exam tip

Remember, some activities that involve hazards are acceptable, because the level of risk is low. For example, whenever we walk along the pavement, road traffic – a significant potential hazard – is very close to us. But the likelihood of actually being harmed by traffic in this situation is low. It would be overly cautious not to let children walk on the pavement. But it is appropriate to minimise the risk – by having a toddler on reins for instance, or holding a child's hand.

Safety equipment

The table below shows key safety equipment that can prevent accidents:

Table 5.1 Key safety equipment

Equipment	Purpose
Harness and reins	Prevent falls from prams, push chairs and high chairs. Prevent young children escaping and/or running into the road when out walking.
Safety gates	Prevent access to kitchens, stairways, outdoors. Always place a guard at the bottom and top of stairs for babies and young children.
Locks for cupboards and windows	Prevent children getting hold of dangerous substances or falling from windows.
Safety glass/safety film	Prevent glass from breaking into pieces, causing injuries.
Socket covers	Prevent children from poking their fingers into electrical sockets.
Play pens	Create a safe area for babies.
Smoke alarms	Detect smoke and sound the alarm.
Cooker guards	Prevent children pulling pans from the cooker.
Firefighting equipment such as fire blankets or extinguishers	May be used to tackle minor fires.

Road safety

- Young children should always be under close and direct supervision of adults when on the pavement or crossing the road.
- You should hold their hand at all times.
- Toddlers are safest on reins.
- Babies and children in prams or buggies should wear a harness.

Follow the Green Cross Code and make children aware of it:

1 First find the safest place to cross.
   - If possible, cross the road at: subways; footbridges; islands; zebra, puffin, pelican or toucan crossings; or where a crossing point is controlled by a police officer, school crossing patrol or traffic warden.
   - Otherwise, choose a place where you can see clearly in all directions, and where drivers can see you.
   - Avoid crossing between parked cars, on sharp bends or close to the top of a hill.
   - There should be space to reach the pavement on the other side.

2 Stop just before you get to the kerb.
   - Do not get too close to the traffic. If there is no pavement, keep back from the edge of the road but make sure you can still see approaching traffic.
   - Give yourself lots of time to have a good look all around.

3 Look all around for traffic and listen.
   - Look in every direction.
   - Listen carefully, because you can sometimes hear traffic before you can see it.

4 If traffic is coming, let it pass.
   - Look all around again and listen.
   - Do not cross until there is a safe gap in the traffic and you are certain that there is plenty of time.
   - Remember, even if traffic is a long way off, it may be approaching very quickly.

5 When it is safe, go straight across the road – do not run.
   - Keep looking and listening for traffic while you cross, in case there is any traffic you did not see, or in case other traffic appears suddenly.
   - Look out for cyclists and motorcyclists travelling between lanes of traffic.
   - Do not cross diagonally.

Now test yourself

TESTED ☐

1 Discuss how to undertake a basic risk assessment of a room used by a young child.
2 Explain the measures you would take to keep a child safe in the bathroom.
3 Outline the five-point Green Cross Code.

5.2 Safety labelling

- Tells you whether a product or piece of equipment is safe for use by children.
- Relevant additional safety information will be specified.
- Always check for safety marks and read safety information before buying or using products for children.

BSI safety mark/kite mark

- This is a UK product and service quality certification mark, administered by the British Standards Institution (BSI).
- It is used to identify products where safety is paramount, for example bicycle helmets and smoke alarms.
- It gives assurance that the product should be safe and reliable
- However, manufacturers are not legally required to display a kite mark on their products.

Figure 5.2 BSI safety mark/kite mark

Lion Mark

- This appears on toys that have been made by a member of the British Toy and Hobby Association and Toy Fair.
- This organisation requires members to sign up to a strict safety Code of Practice.
- Around 95 per cent of toys sold in the UK are supplied with a Lion Mark, as many major UK and European toy manufacturers are members.

Figure 5.3 Lion Mark

Revision activity

Read more about safety labelling and selecting safe items in Unit R019 of the textbook, page 91.

Age advice symbol

- This identifies when equipment or a product isn't suitable for children under the age of 36 months (in the opinion of the manufacturer).
- It is mainly displayed on toys that might not pass a 'choke hazard test'.
- It is also seen if a product has small parts that could be removed and swallowed by children under three years.

Figure 5.4 Age advice symbol

CE symbol

- Most common toy label and the first one to look for.
- By law, it has to be displayed on all new toys on the market in the EU.
- The CE logo proves that the toy has been tested for compliance with EU standards.
- It is also the manufacturer's declaration that the item meets all toy safety requirements.

Figure 5.5 CE symbol

Children's nightwear labelling

- Nightwear can burn quickly if set alight by contact with an open fire, gas or electric fire, or another heat source.
- This can cause serious injury.
- You should look for a label confirming that children's night garments (including dressing gowns) meet the flammability performance requirements.
- This includes garments for babies.
- Stretch garments, such as baby grows, should be treated as children's nightwear.

> **Revision activity**
>
> When out shopping, study the labelling on a few pieces of children's and babies' nightwear. This will enable you to become familiar with the real thing.

Now test yourself

TESTED ☐

1 Discuss the safety marks you should look for when buying toys.
2 Explain why the CE Mark is the most common toy label and the first one to look for.
3 Outline the garments for babies and children on which you should look for children's nightwear labelling.

5.3 Be aware of the most common childhood accidents

Note that the information in this section by no means replaces first aid training.

- All practitioners should take a paediatric first aid course.
- It is important to recognise when medical assistance is urgently required, as this can save a child's life.

The most common childhood accidents are shown in Figure 5.6.

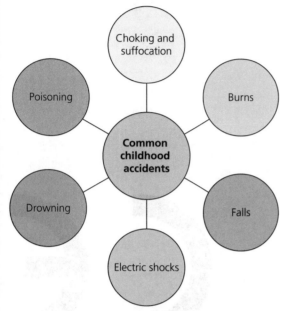

Figure 5.6 Common childhood accidents

Choking and suffocation

- Babies and children can choke to death on any small object they put in their mouths that blocks their airway.
- You must be very careful which objects are left within reach.
- Children can also struggle to breathe or stop breathing due to suffocation.
- This can happen when the airway is blocked externally.
- Choking on food is also common.

Mild or severe obstruction

- If there is a minor airway obstruction, breathing will be difficult, but the child will still be able to get some air into their lungs.
- They will be able to cough.
- With difficulty, they will also be able to talk, cry or make a noise.
- If obstruction is severe, the child will not be able to do these things.
- They may hold their neck.
- Not being able to breathe will eventually cause the child to lose consciousness.
- Therefore, immediate treatment is needed and you must call an ambulance.

> **Common mistake**
>
> You will know how to call the emergency services from a landline – by dialling 999. But do not forget that from a mobile, the number to call is 112.

First aid for a choking child

- Encourage the child to cough, as this could clear the obstruction.
- If the obstruction is severe and the child can't breathe – or if coughing fails – bend the child forwards and give up to five sharp back blows between the shoulder blades with the heel of the hand.
- Check the mouth and remove any obvious obstruction.
- If the child is still choking, administer abdominal thrusts – stand behind the child and put your fist between the navel and the lower breastbone, grasp the fist with the other hand and pull sharply in an upwards and inwards movement, up to five times.
- Recheck the mouth as before.
- If the child is still choking, alternate between back blows and abdominal thrusts until the airway is cleared, emergency help arrives or the child becomes unconscious.

First aid for a choking infant

- Lie the infant along the forearm on its front, keeping the head low.
- Take care to support the head.
- Give the infant up to five sharp back blows between the shoulder blades with the heel of the hand.
- Turn the infant onto its back along the other arm.
- Check the mouth and remove any obvious obstruction.
- If the infant is still choking, administer chest thrusts. With two fingertips, give up to five sharp thrusts on the lower part of the breastbone (a finger's breadth below the nipples), pressing inwards and upwards.
- Recheck the mouth as before.
- If the infant is still choking, alternate between back blows and chest thrusts until the airway is cleared, emergency help arrives or the infant becomes unconscious.

Burns

The causes of burns and scalds are shown in Figure 5.7.

First aid for burns and scalds

- Burns and scalds need immediate treatment. This can limit their effect.
- An infant or young child with any burn needs to go to hospital straight away.
- Cool the area with water for at least ten minutes, preferably by holding it under gently running tap water.
- Remove any jewellery, watches, belts or restrictive clothing that isn't stuck to the burn/scald before swelling occurs.
- Cover the burn/scald with clean cling film or place a clean plastic bag over a foot or hand.
- Cling film should be applied lengthways instead of being wrapped around a limb due to the risk of swelling.
- If cling film/bags are not available, a sterile dressing may be used.
- Blister plasters must not be used on burn/ scald blisters
- Blisters should not be broken or the injured skin interfered with.
- Do not apply fats such as butter.

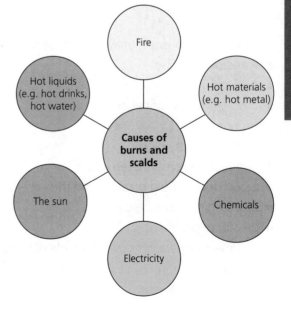

Figure 5.7 The causes of burns and scalds

Falls

- Falls injuries are common
- They can occur as a result of a seemingly minor trip or slip.
- Fractures and head injuries are the most common fall injuries.
- Adults should fit window locks and stair gates, and supervise carefully whenever there is a risk of falling.

Head injuries

It is important to recognise head injuries as they:

- are common and can be serious
- can result in impaired consciousness or unconsciousness
- may require emergency surgery.

The following head injuries may occur:

- Concussion – caused when a brain is shaken within the skull, usually by a blow to the head. Normal brain activity is disturbed temporarily, but is usually followed by a complete recovery.
- Cerebral compression – occurs when pressure builds up on the brain.
  - This is usually a result of swelling of injured brain tissue or a build-up of blood within the skull, caused by a blow to the head.
  - It can also be caused by an infection, brain tumour or stroke.
  - Surgery is generally required to relieve the pressure.
  - Prolonged pressure can cause disability and death.
- Skull fracture – this is a break in the skull, caused by a blow to the head.

Figure 5.8 Stair gates protect young children from falls.

Signs and symptoms

These include:

- bump or other swelling
- bruising
- headache
- drowsiness
- loss of consciousness (may only last seconds)
- vomiting or nausea
- confusion/loss of memory
- dizziness or loss of balance
- seizures
- problems with vision
- pupils of the eyes uneven in size
- blood or clear fluid coming from the nose or ear
- bleeding from the head
- breathing problems
- weakness or paralysis down one side of the face or body
- difficulties talking
- change in behaviour

- a change in the sound of their cry (babies only)
- swollen fontanelle (babies only).

First aid for head injuries

- Call for an ambulance.
- Apply a pad and direct pressure to any head wound.
- Lie the casualty down. See below if a spinal injury is suspected.
- Monitor and record the level of consciousness, breathing and pulse until the ambulance arrives.
- Also record symptoms, including how long any loss of consciousness lasted, if blood or fluid has leaked from the nose/ear, pupil size, any vomiting, etc.

Protecting the spinal cord

- People with head injuries often also injure their neck (which is part of the spine).
- If the spinal cord becomes damaged due to broken or dislocated bones in the spine, paralysis and other serious conditions may occur.
- A first aider will treat an unconscious casualty with a head injury as though they also have a spinal injury, to prevent them from causing further damage.

Signs and symptoms of spinal injury include:
- neck or back pain
- abnormal curve of the spine
- loss of sensation
- abnormal sensation
- weakness in or inability to move limbs
- skin feels tender
- loss of bladder/bowel control
- breathing difficulties.

First aid for spinal injury or an unconscious child

- Do not move the child/tell the child not to move.
- Kneel behind them and place steady hands on either side of their face. Steadily support the neck and head. Keep holding in place until the ambulance arrives.
- For extra support, get others to place padding such as rolled up blankets around the neck and shoulders (without moving the child).

Electric shocks

- Electricity can be extremely dangerous
- Electric shocks can kill by stopping the heart.
- It is important to fit socket covers that protect children.
- If a child has been electrocuted, stop the flow of electricity before approaching, or you are likely to receive an electric shock.
- Turn off power at the mains/master switch.
- If turning off power is impossible, the child may be pushed or pulled well away from the source using a material that will not conduct the electricity.

Common mistake

It is common to forget that cerebral compression can develop hours or days after a head injury. A child with a banged head should be watched closely for at least six hours. Adults should remain alert for the signs of head injury for several days.

- A first aider will learn how to do this safely on a first aid course (e.g. looping a thick towel around the feet to enable a child to be pulled from the source, or using a wooden broom to push them away).

First aid for electric shocks

- Once safe, approach the child.
- If the heart has stopped, an ambulance is needed.
- Check the airway, breathing and circulation and start **CPR**.
- Electricity can cause burns at the entry and exit points, which must be treated with cold water.
- Water and electricity are a very dangerous combination. So be sure the electricity source is off/the child is far enough away from it.
- Urgent or emergency medical attention will be needed, depending on the extent and severity of the burns.

Drowning

- Occurs in natural water bodies, such as the sea and rivers.
- Can also happen in manmade places, such as pools, canals, lakes, ponds and baths.

First aid for drowning

- Carry the child out of the water with their head lower than their chest.
- Take off their wet clothing.
- Cover them with a dry towel/blanket.
- If they are unconscious and breathing, put them into the **recovery position**.
- If they are not breathing, give CPR.

Poisoning

Poisons enter the body when they:

- are swallowed (bleach or berries, etc.)
- come into contact with the skin (poison ivy, etc.)
- are inhaled (poisonous gas fumes or dust such as ant powder, etc.).

Some common household/workplace substances and plants can poison children, and it is important to guard against this. Common items include:

- cleaning fluids/sprays
- medication and prescription drugs
- personal care products/make-up
- pesticides
- some plants, including delphinium, mistletoe, wild mushrooms and other fungi, foxgloves, daffodil bulbs, poison ivy
- berries from bushes and trees should all be regarded as poisonous because it is difficult to tell which are which.

CPR – cardiopulmonary resuscitation, sometimes referred to as 'heart massage and rescue breaths'.

Common mistake

Don't forget that babies and young children can drown in as little as 2.5 cm of water, which is enough to cover their face should they fall forwards. Never leave a baby or young child unattended anywhere near water, even for a few seconds.

Recovery position – a safe position in which to place an unconscious, breathing child.

Figure 5.9 Never leave a baby or young child unattended anywhere near water.

Signs and symptoms of poisoning

These vary according to what the poison is and how it has been ingested; they include:

- vomiting
- pain
- drowsiness or unconsciousness
- burns to mouth (if chemicals have been swallowed)
- blisters on skin
- swelling
- itchy skin and/or severe rash
- unusual smell on the breath.

Other evidence may also be present:

- smells (gas fumes, bleach, etc.)
- spilt poisonous liquids
- open chemical containers, such as cleaning fluid bottles
- open/empty medication blister packs or medicine/pill bottles
- open medicine cabinet
- open cleaning cupboard
- berries or pieces of plant in the vicinity of the child.

First aid for poisoning

- Call an ambulance straight away.
- Try to find out what substance or plant the child has taken or been in contact with, how much they have taken and when.
- Pass this information to emergency services.
- If a substance or plant has been touched, rinse it from the skin with running tap water.
- Monitor closely, and be ready to act if the child becomes unconscious. (If they do, check the airway, breathing and circulation, place the child in the recovery position and continue to monitor them until help arrives.)
- Never try to get a child who has been poisoned to vomit.

Now test yourself

1 Discuss what you would do if a child in your care received an electric shock.
2 Explain the circumstances in which a child could be at risk of drowning.
3 Outline the treatment that should be given to a child who has been scalded.

5.4 Social safety

Adults need to teach children:

- about their rights in respect of their bodies
- what to do if they are in an emergency situation and they are vulnerable
- what to do if they are bullied.

Personal safety awareness

- Knowing what to do in an emergency situation helps keep children safe.
- It also helps them to develop confidence and self-reliance.
- This makes then less likely to become a victim of abuse.

Children should know what to do if they are lost:

- Stop and look all around for the adult they are with.
- If they can't see them, they should approach a safe person – a police officer, CPO, crossing point patrol guard (lollipop person), cashier at a till in a shop or, lastly, a parent with children.
- They should wait outside until their adult, parent or a police officer comes to look after them. They should not go anywhere with strangers.

Children should also know:

- who to go home with when away from their parent
- never to answer the door alone
- personal details – their full name, address and telephone number.

Figure 5.10 Children should know who they can go home with.

Awareness of strangers

- Children need to know what a stranger is, and what to do if they are approached.
- If an unknown person talks to them, they need not be rude – they can walk away quickly, telling an adult if they feel worried.
- If a stranger asks or tells a child to go with them, the child should run away and tell a safe adult immediately.
- They must learn to 'Say no, never go!'
- If children are touched, grabbed or feel frightened or worried that they are in danger, it is alright to break the usual behaviour rules.
- They should attract attention by shouting and screaming, and punch and kick, if they feel they need to.

Avoiding inappropriate personal contact – physical and emotional

- Teach children that their bodies and feelings are their own.
- It is wrong for them to be touched in a way that hurts them, frightens them or feels rude.
- They should tell a safe adult if they are worried about this or it occurs.
- They do not have to show physical affection to anyone if they do not want to (kissing, hugging, sitting on laps).
- Children can have help if they need it when toileting, but they have a right to privacy if they want it.
- Children should know that it is wrong for them to be bullied.
- They should tell a safe adult if they are worried about this or it occurs.

Internet safety

- By the age of five, most children use computers.
- Via family members, they are likely to have access to a mobile phone/ games console with internet connection.

Dangers

The possible dangers of using technology include:

- Physical danger/contact with strangers who may seek to harm a child – these people may pose as a child online and pretend to have similar interests.
  - They may then use this to establish an online 'friendship'.
  - When trust has developed, they may entice the child to meet up with them in person.
  - This is known as **child grooming**.
- Exposure to inappropriate material – this may be pornographic, violent, hateful or promote dangerous or illegal behaviour, or it may simply be inappropriate for the child's age.
- Divulging personal details (may be used in identity theft or fraud).
- Illegal behaviour – including illegally downloading copyrighted material.
- Attempting to buy things online – including in-app purchases.
- **Cyberbullying** – can leave victims extremely upset, scared and humiliated.

> **Child grooming** – occurs when someone establishes an online 'friendship' with a child, intending to entice them to meet up when trust has developed.
>
> **Cyberbullying** – occurs when a child is bullied online, for example in a chat room or via social media.

Talking to children about internet use and how to be safe

- It is important that young children understand the dangers of the internet and how to enjoy it safely.
- Adults should to talk to children about this, answer their questions and put precautions in place to protect them.

Safety strategies

- Young children should be made aware of child-friendly search engines.
- Alternatively, safe search settings can be turned on to allow safe use of traditional search engines.

Children should also be told not to:

- give out personal information, (name, home address, landline and mobile numbers, bank details, PINs and passwords, etc.)
- supply registration details without asking for permission and help
- visit chat websites or social networking sites without asking for permission and help
- arrange to meet an online friend in person without parental knowledge and permission (if a parent agrees to let them, they should always go along with them)
- give any indication of their age or sex in a personal email address or screen name
- keep anything that worries or upsets them online secret from you
- respond to unwanted emails or other messages.

> **Common mistake**
>
> Don't fall into the trap of thinking that giving children guidelines is enough. It is also good practice to monitor children's internet use by checking the history folder on the browser regularly. This contains a list of sites that have been visited.

Explore sites and apps together

- This is a great way to teach children how to use technology.
- It gives you the opportunity to talk about safe use together.
- While guiding children, you can satisfy yourself that the sites/apps are appropriate.

Family discussions

- The whole family should be aware of how to keep children safe online.
- This is especially true if there are older siblings in the home who may be accessing content that is not appropriate for younger children.

If a child comes across something that upsets, worries or shocks them online, discuss it and give plenty of reassurance. Talking through how to avoid a repeat incident will help a child to rebuild their confidence. Parents are advised to:

- contact their internet service provider if a child comes across inappropriate content or is subjected to any inappropriate contact while online
- report any worries about illegal materials or suspicious behaviour to the Child Exploitation and Online Protection Centre (www.ceop.police.uk)
- install and regularly update filtering software to protect against inappropriate internet access.

Figure 5.11 **Explore websites and apps together.**

Agree boundaries

Parents should create clear rules for internet use with the child, such as:

- The internet-connected computer must be in a family room with the screen facing outward so you can see what is happening.
- If a child accidentally goes to an unsuitable website, they should tell you. This can then be deleted from the 'history' folder and you can add the address to the 'parental control' filter list.
- The child should take breaks from the computer every 30 minutes for health and safety reasons.
- The child should not download files from the internet without your agreement – it is best to never download unknown files at all.
- Children should not download or share files illegally (music, films, etc.).
- Children should not attempt to buy or order things online.

Using safe search facilities and restrictions

- Adults should always use the parental controls available on computers, tablets, games consoles and mobile phones.
- These help to keep children safe by:
  - blocking inappropriate websites and email addresses by adding them to a filter list
  - setting time limits for the use of computers and devices
  - preventing children from searching certain words.

Now test yourself

TESTED

1 Discuss how you can help a child to keep themselves safe from stranger danger.
2 Outline the internet rules you would introduce to protect a child.
3 Explain the action a child should take if they are lost.

Success in the examination

The written exam

REVISED

Unit R018 is an examined unit where you will sit an examination paper that is set and marked by the OCR examinations board.

In the exam, you will be tested on five Learning Objectives (LOs):

1 Understand reproduction and the roles and responsibilities of parenthood
2 Understand antenatal care and preparation for birth
3 Understand postnatal checks, postnatal provision and conditions for development
4 Understand how to recognise, manage and prevent childhood illnesses
5 Know about child safety.

Questions might be about a particular LO topic or might require answers that combine information from two or more different LOs.

How long will I have to complete the exam?

The examination will last for 1 hour and 15 minutes. It will be conducted under examination conditions.

What type of questions will appear in the exam paper?

- The question paper consists of two sections, comprising short answer and extended response questions.
- During the external assessment, you will be expected to demonstrate your understanding by answering questions that require the skills of analysis and evaluation in particular contexts.
- All of the questions will have a 'command verb'. This will tell you what you have to do to answer the question. Examples of command verbs are shown below. You will find a Marking criteria glossary of terms in the centre handbook on the OCR website.

Examples of command verbs

Command verb	Meaning
Describe	Set out characteristics
Discuss	Present, explain and evaluate salient points (e.g. for/against an argument)
Explain	Set out the purposes or reasons
Evaluate	Make a qualitative judgement, taking into account different factors and using available knowledge/ experience
List	Document a series of outcomes, events or information

Always check the command verb carefully before answering a question. If you **describe** something when the question asks you to **explain**, you will not be able to gain full marks. This is because an explanation requires more detail than a description.

You will find a Marking criteria glossary of terms, which includes all the command verbs and definitions, in the centre handbook on the OCR website.

Exam technique top tips!

- Do not open the exam paper until you are instructed to do so.
- Read the information on the front of the paper.
- Make sure you use the correct colour pen.
- Read the paper all the way through first, then start work on a question to which you know the answer.
- Before answering a question, read it through twice, to be absolutely sure you understand the answer required.
- Pay close attention to the command verbs. Underline or highlight the command verb so that you are clear about what you have to do.
- Looking at the marks available will help you to see how many answers or points are required.
- If a question asks for 'ways', without saying how many ways, you must give a minimum of two ways, because 'ways' is plural. The same rule applies to 'methods', 'reasons' and so on.
- Make sure the information in your answer is accurate and relevant to the question. Don't just write everything you know about a topic – stay focused and answer the question!
- If you don't know an answer, do your best to answer anyway: you might just pick up extra points.
- Be guided by the number of marks and the space provided for the length of your answer. The more marks, the more space will be provided. Unless you have very large handwriting, you should not need to continue your answer on the extra pages at the end of the examination paper.
- If you do continue your answers on the extra pages, make sure you state the question number and the part of the question, for example 3(b) or 6(a), so that the examiner marking your paper knows exactly which question you are answering.

Preparing for the exam

- Find the past papers and mark schemes on the OCR website. Have a go at a paper, then mark it yourself using the mark scheme.
- Always ask your teacher if you don't understand something or are not sure. Your teacher is there to help you.
- Make a revision schedule and stick to it. It should be a timetable with dates.
- It is never too early to start revising. Begin your revision by going through your handouts and notes after each lesson – don't just file them away!
- You can use the revision planner at the front of this book and tick off each topic after you have revised it.
- Use the revision activities suggested in this book, so that you don't get bored just reading through notes all the time.
- Learn the key terms for each topic, so that you are able to use specialist terminology correctly in your answers.
- Get a good night's sleep the night before the exam.
- Be sure to eat breakfast and lunch on the day of the exam, and drink plenty of water: this will help you to concentrate.
- If you feel nervous, take a few deep breaths.

Sample practice questions and commentary

LO1: Understand reproduction and the roles and responsibilities of parenthood

Sample exam question

Shaun and Amina intend to start trying for a baby within the next few months.

a) Explain two areas of pre-conception health which Amina should consider before trying to conceive.

Mark scheme and additional guidance

Expected answers	Marks	Additional guidance
Two explanations required, two marks each: • Diet • Exercise • Healthy weight • Smoking/alcohol/ recreational drugs • Up-to-date immunisations	**4** (2 × 2)	Two marks: the chosen area of pre-conception health clearly considered. One mark: simple identification of an area of pre-conception health, with limited or no explanation.

Sample answer

1. Amina should consider the dangers of smoking, alcohol and recreational drugs, as these can cause very serious damage to an unborn child. A foetus needs protection from these.

2. She should also eat well.

Commentary

Question context/content/style

Explanation of two considerations of pre-conception health. Four marks.

Requirements

Limited, correct explanation of two considerations of pre-conception health.

Marks awarded and rationale: 2/4

- The first answer is correctly identified and explained, gaining two marks.
- The second answer is not sufficient to credit any marks, as it is too vague and could apply to anyone.

Sample exam question

b) Some methods of contraception are shown in the box below.

Female condom	Combined pill	Diaphragm

Complete the table to match each method of delivery with the brief description given.

Method of delivery	Description
	Dome-shaped piece of latex or silicone that covers the cervix. It is inserted into the vagina before sex, and must be used alongside spermicidal gel or cream, which will kill sperm.
	A sheath made from polyurethane. It is put inside the vagina before it comes into contact with the penis.
	Contains hormones that prevent pregnancy. The woman takes this for 21 days, then has a break for seven days.

Mark scheme and additional guidance

Expected answers	Marks	Additional guidance
Three matches required, one mark each. The answers should appear in the table in the correct order: • Diaphragm • Female condom • Combined pill	3 (3 × 1)	

Sample answer

Method of delivery	Description
Female condom	Dome-shaped piece of latex or silicone that covers the cervix. It is inserted into the vagina before sex, and must be used alongside spermicidal gel or cream, which will kill sperm.
Diaphragm	A sheath made from polyurethane. It is put inside the vagina before it comes into contact with the penis.
Combined pill	Contains hormones that prevent pregnancy. The woman takes this for 21 days, then has a break for seven days.

Commentary

Question context/content/style

Match the method of conception with the brief descriptions given.

Requirements:

Correct matching of three methods of conception with their brief descriptions.

Marks awarded and rationale: 1/3

- The third method of contraception has been matched correctly, gaining one mark.
- The first and second methods of contraception have not been matched correctly, so no marks are gained.

LO2: Understand antenatal care and preparation for birth

Sample exam question

a) Complete the table by naming the routine checks carried out at an antenatal clinic, including scans. The first one has been done for you. Fill in **five** more.

Routine checks	Routine scans
weight check	

Mark scheme and additional guidance

Expected answers	Marks	Additional guidance
Five required, **one** mark each: • Blood tests • Blood pressure • Urine test • STIs • Examination of the uterus • Baby's heartbeat • Ultrasound dating scan	**5** (5 × 1)	The question asks for routine checks, so the names of specialised diagnostic tests will not receive marks.

Sample answer

Routine checks	Routine scans
weight check	ultrasound dating scan
blood pressure	
urine test	
STI tests	
pregnancy test	

Commentary

Question context/content/style:

Naming of five routine checks carried out at an antenatal clinic, including scans. Five marks.

Requirements:

Correct naming of the routine checks carried out at an antenatal clinic, including scans.

Marks awarded and rationale: 4/5

- Four correct routine checks/scans have been explained, gaining four marks.
- The answer 'pregnancy test' is incorrect, so no marks are awarded.

Sample exam question

b) Complete the table to describe two different methods of delivery. An example has been done for you.

Method of delivery	Description
Ventouse	A plastic or metal cup is fitted firmly on the baby's head by suction. As the mother pushes, an obstetrician gently pulls to help deliver the baby.

Mark scheme and additional guidance

Expected answers	Marks	Additional guidance
Two required, **one** mark for each name and one mark for each correct description. • Forceps • Caesarean section	4 (2 × 2)	One mark for identifying a method of delivery, and one mark for a limited explanation of it.

Sample answer

Method of delivery	Description
Ventouse	A plastic or metal cup is fitted firmly on the baby's head by suction. As the mother pushes, an obstetrician gently pulls to help deliver the baby.
Forceps	A curved metal instrument fits carefully around the baby's head. As the mother pushes, an obstetrician gently pulls to help deliver the baby.
Caesarean section	This is an operation to deliver the baby through a cut made in the abdomen and womb of the mother.

Commentary

Question context/content/style:

Name and describe two methods of delivery.

Requirements:

Correct identification of two methods of delivery and brief descriptions of them.

Marks awarded and rationale: 4/4

- Both answers are correct.

LO3: Understand postnatal checks, postnatal provision and conditions for development

Sample exam question

a) Describe why pre-term babies often have breathing and feeding problems.

Mark scheme and additional guidance

Expected answers	Marks	Additional guidance
Two descriptions are required: one for breathing problems and one for feeding problems; **two** marks each	4 (2 × 2)	For each problem: **Two marks** for a full, realistic description **One mark** for a limited description

Sample answer

In pre-term babies, the lungs are often not mature enough to adjust after birth, so help is needed. Healthcare professionals will provide help that is as gentle as possible, because ventilators can cause lung problems.

If there's a gap in the roof of the mouth, the baby has a 'cleft palate'. This makes feeding hard, and surgery is needed. If a baby has persistent problems latching on during breastfeeding, they may have 'tongue-tie'. The baby might need a very simple procedure that generally overcomes feeding problems immediately. It is very common for parents to experience issues with feeding at some point. So, information, advice and support are needed.

Commentary

Question context/content/style:

Descriptions of breathing problems and feeding problems are given.

Requirements:

- Correct description of breathing problems given.
- Correct description of feeding problems given.

Marks awarded and rationale: 4/4

- The answers are correct and both gain two marks giving a total of four marks.

Sample exam question

b) Suggest **three** checks that will be carried out by a health visitor or doctor during a postnatal check.

Mark scheme and additional guidance

Expected answers	Marks	Additional guidance
Three examples required, one mark each: • Apgar score • Skin • Birthmarks • Weight • Length • Head circumference • Fontanelle • Eyes • Mouth • Feet • Fingers • Hips • Reflexes	**3** (3 × 1)	

Sample answer

1. The baby's reflexes will be tested.

2. The hips will be checked for developmental dysplasia.

3. The baby will be weighed.

Commentary

Question context/content/style:

Three checks made at the postnatal check are given.

Requirements:

Correct description of three checks made at the postnatal check.

Marks awarded and rationale: 3/3

● The answers are correct and each gain one mark giving a total of three marks.

Sample exam question

c) Postnatal checks are carried out on newborn babies. Give **four** reflexes medical professionals will normally expect to see.

Mark scheme and additional guidance

Expected answers	Marks	Additional guidance
Four required, **one** mark each. • Sucking • Rooting • Grasp • Walking • Startle (Moro)	**4** (4 × 1)	The command word 'give' indicates that a simple one-word response is sufficient for each example.

Sample answer

1. Sucking

2. Rooting

3. Grasp

4. Startle

Commentary

Question context/content/style:

Four reflexes medical professionals normally expect to see during postnatal checks. Four marks.

Requirements:

Correct names of four reflexes.

Marks awarded and rationale: 4/4

• Four reflexes have been named correctly, gaining four marks.

Sample exam question

Marnie often has tantrums at bedtime in particular.

d) Identify and explain two ways in which Marnie's parents could promote positive behaviour at home.

Your answer must:

○ Include examples of what they could do

○ Explain how your examples can help promote positive behaviour.

Mark scheme and additional guidance

Expected answers	Marks	Additional guidance
Examples of what Marnie's parents could do: • Notice and praise good behaviour • Use a reward chart linked to a behaviour goal • Role model positive behaviour • Talk through situations with Marnie • Set boundaries for behaviour **How these promote positive behaviour:** • Children enjoy praise and feel proud of themselves • Reward charts give a visual reminder • If the child repeats good behaviour, it will become a habit • Talking about and explaining the situation helps the child think it through • Consistent boundaries help the child understand what is not allowed	8	Do not credit examples of what the parents should **not** do. **Level 3 (7–8 marks):** • Detailed explanation • Clear, logical line of reasoning • Two or more examples • High QWC, with few errors, if any **Level 2 (4–6 marks)** • Sound explanation • At least two examples • A line of reasoning, with some structure • Information given is mostly relevant • Mid QWC: there may be some errors **Level 1 (1–3 marks)** • Basic description with little or no explanation (list-like answers will be marked at this level) • May not be specific to Marnie's situation • Answers may be muddled, demonstrating little knowledge or understanding • Low QWC: errors may be very noticeable **0 marks:** response not worthy of credit

Sample answer

Marnie's parents should praise her when she behaves well. Children feel proud when adults notice and praise specific positive behaviour. They enjoy the approval and feel encouraged to repeat the behaviour, until it becomes a normal, everyday part of what they do. Verbal praise is the most effective.

They could use a reward chart relating to her behaviour at bedtime. Sometimes a reward chart can be an effective visual reward system.

Commentary

Question context/content/style:

Suggestions for promoting positive behaviour and explanations.

Requirements:

Correct suggestions and explanations given, linked to Marnie's situation.

Marks awarded and rationale: 5/8

• A sound explanation with two relevant examples, although it would need more detail and depth to reach the top of Level 2 (6 marks).

• The answer could be more detailed to reach Level 3.

LO4: Understand how to recognise, manage and prevent childhood illnesses

Sample exam question

c) State **three** ways by which you could support a child who will soon be experiencing his or her first hospital stay.

Mark scheme and additional guidance

Expected answers	Marks	Additional guidance
Three ways identified, **one** mark each. • Visit the hospital ward they will be on, to meet the doctor and nurses • Acting out fears and playing hospital games • Books and DVDs about being in hospital • Explanation and honesty • Arrange to be involved in his or her care	**3** (3 × 1)	Do not accept 'books and DVDs' unless it is specified that they relate to the hospital.

Sample answer

1. Acting out fears and playing hospital games.

2. Books and DVDs.

3. Talking honestly about what will happen.

Commentary

Question context/content/style:

Identification of three ways in which a child who will soon be experiencing his or her first hospital stay can be supported.

Requirements:

Correct identification of three methods.

Marks awarded and rationale: 2/3

● Three suggestions are given, but 'books and DVDs' is not very specific.

Sample exam question

b) Some diet-related illnesses are shown in the box below.

Food allergies	Childhood obesity	Diabetes

Complete the table to match each illness with the brief description given.

Diet-related illness	Description
	The body doesn't produce the hormone insulin, which affects the body's ability to process the sugar or glucose in food.
	Common examples of this include nuts, eggs, shellfish. In the most severe cases there may be anaphylactic shock – a life-threatening situation.
	This means becoming very overweight and can lead to other health problems.

Mark scheme and additional guidance

Expected answers	Marks	Additional guidance
Three required, **one** mark each.	**3**	
The answers should appear in the table in the following order: • Diabetes • Food allergies • Childhood obesity	(3 × 1)	

Sample answer

Diet-related illness	Description
Diabetes	The body doesn't produce the hormone insulin, which affects the body's ability to process the sugar or glucose in food.
Food allergies	Common examples of this include nuts, eggs, shellfish. In the most severe cases there may be anaphylactic shock – a life-threatening situation.
Childhood obesity	This means becoming very overweight and can lead to other health problems.

Commentary

Question context/content/style:
Match the diet-related illnesses with the brief descriptions given.

Requirements:
Correct matching of three diet-related illnesses with their brief descriptions.

Marks awarded and rationale: 3/3

● Three diet-related illnesses have been matched, gaining three marks.

LO5: Know about child safety

Sample exam question

a) Identify **three** appropriate boundaries you could agree with a child to help to keep them safe online.

Mark scheme and additional guidance

Expected answers	Marks	Additional guidance
Three required, one mark each The following are all acceptable: • Only using child-friendly search engines or traditional search engines with safe settings turned on. • Not giving out personal information (e.g. name, address, phone numbers, passwords). • Not supplying online registration details without asking for permission and help. • Not visiting chat websites or social networking sites without asking for permission and help. • Not arranging to meet an online friend in person without parental knowledge and permission. • Not giving any indication of their age or sex in a personal email address or screen name. • Not keep anything that worries or upsets them online secret from you or their parents. • Not responding to unwanted emails or other messages, but telling you/their parents about them. • Not having computers, iPads or other devices in their bedroom. • Placing the computer in an open area of the house where their parents can see the screen.	3 (3 × 1)	

Sample answer

1. The child should only use safe search engines. The safe settings on a general search engine can be switched on, or a special child-friendly search engine can be used. Then only age-appropriate content will be seen.

2. The child should never give out their personal details, including their name, age, date of birth, home address, telephone numbers and passwords.

3. Children shouldn't have email addresses.

Commentary

Question context/content/style:

Identification of three appropriate boundaries that could be agreed with a child to help keep them safe online.

Requirements:

Three correct examples given.

Marks awarded and rationale: 2/3

- The first two answers are correct, gaining one mark each.
- The third answer is incorrect and does not gain a mark.

Sample exam question

b) Name three common childhood accidents.

Mark scheme and additional guidance

Expected answers	Marks	Additional guidance
Three required, one mark each: • Choking and suffocation • Burns • Falls • Electric shocks • Drowning • Poisoning	3 (3 × 1)	

> **Sample answer**
>
> 1. Burns
> 2. Falls
> 3. Drowning

Commentary

Question context/content/style:

Identification of three common childhood accidents.

Requirements:

Correct common childhood accidents given.

Marks awarded and rationale: 3/3

- Three correct answers have been given.

Glossary

Amnion – closed sac in which the baby develops in the womb; contains amniotic fluid.

Amniotic fluid – the fluid that surrounds the baby in the womb.

Anaphylactic shock – a severe allergic reaction, and a life-threatening situation.

Antenatal care – the care received by a woman during her pregnancy.

Antibodies – proteins made by the body that can latch on to foreign viruses and bacteria, making them ineffective.

Apgar score – score given to evaluate the physical condition of a newborn on assessment of their vital signs.

Barrier method – a method of contraception in which a device or preparation prevents sperm from reaching an egg.

Caesarean – when a baby is delivered through a surgical incision (cut) made in the mother's abdomen and uterus.

Child grooming – occurs when someone establishes an online 'friendship' with a child, intending to entice them to meet up when trust has developed.

Chromosomal abnormalities – occur when a portion of chromosomal DNA is irregular, missing or duplicated.

CPR – cardiopulmonary resuscitation, sometimes referred to as 'heart massage and rescue breaths'.

Cyberbullying – occurs when a child is bullied online, for example in a chat room or via social media.

Genetic disorders – disorders inherited from one or both parents.

Hazard – an item or situation that may cause harm.

Hepatitis – virus that can cause liver disease. There are five 'types' of viral hepatitis – A, B, C, D and E.

HIV – human immunodeficiency virus. It is spread through bodily fluids, and attacks the body's immune system, weakening the ability to fight everyday illnesses.

Hormonal method – a method of contraception in which hormones prevent eggs from being released from the ovaries, thicken cervical mucus to prevent sperm from entering the uterus, and thin the lining of the uterus to prevent implantation.

Immunity – when an organism has the ability to resist disease.

Ketones – produced when the body burns fat for energy. They are also produced when someone loses weight or when the body is lacking the sufficient insulin to use sugar for energy.

Menopause – when a woman stops having a reproductive cycle.

Placenta – flat, round organ in the womb of a pregnant woman that supplies the baby with all the oxygen, food and nutrients it needs.

Postnatal – relating to or denoting the period after the birth of a baby.

Postnatal care – the care received by a woman following the birth of her baby.

Pre-eclampsia – a condition in which a woman has high levels of protein in her urine. Swelling in the feet, legs and hands is also common. If left untreated, eclampsia can develop, which can be very harmful to mother and baby. Symptoms of eclampsia include seizures in the mother.

Pre-term – a baby born before week 37 of pregnancy (also called 'premature').

Primary needs – the basic needs that must be met in order for a child to survive.

Recovery position – a safe position in which to place an unconscious, breathing child.

Risk – the likelihood of a hazard actually causing harm.

Role model – someone who demonstrates how to behave by example.

The Food Standards Agency – a government department that issues guidelines on healthy eating.

Transition stage – this links the end of the first stage of labour and the beginning of the second stage of labour.

Umbilical cord – flexible cord-like structure that connects the baby to the mother's placenta while in the womb.

Vaccine/vaccination – a biological preparation that provides or improves immunity to a specific disease, commonly given via an injection.

Now test yourself answers

1.1 The wide range of factors that affect the decision to have children

1. Three from: the relationship between partners; finance; parental age; peer pressure/social expectations; genetic counselling for hereditary diseases.

2. Finance is an important consideration because raising a child is very expensive. Research shows that the average costs are rising. The most expensive years are between the ages of one and four.

3. Older parents are more likely to be financially secure. This can be a big advantage, as raising a child is very expensive. Older parents are also more likely to be mature, relaxed and confident about parenthood. This may be down to their increased life experience, which in turn increases their ability to handle challenges. They may have already established a career, and completed training/qualifications before starting a family. Gaining these things can be harder when children come along because of the increased family demands on time.

4. Two from: if parents already have a child who has a genetic disorder or congenital defect; if there is family history of birth defects, genetic disorders or some forms of cancer; if there have been repeated miscarriages or problems getting pregnant; if there is a blood relationship between the partners (for example, cousins); if a parent's ethnic background is one in which genetic disorders are more likely.

1.2 Pre-conception health

1. Three from: diet; exercise; healthy weight; smoking/alcohol/recreational drugs; up-to-date immunisations.

2. The baby is reliant on the mother for all the nutrients needed for growth and development. So when the mother eats healthily and gets the correct nutrients, the baby benefits. A healthy diet is also vital for the mother's health during pregnancy.

3. If a mother drinks alcohol in pregnancy, it enters the mother's bloodstream and is passed to the baby via the placenta. This can seriously affect the development of the baby's liver, increase the likelihood of premature birth and low birth weight and if drinking is heavy, cause foetal alcohol syndrome. Regular or binge drinking is very dangerous. There is debate over how much alcohol is safe for a pregnant mother to drink, but the more a woman drinks, the higher the risk to her baby, so the best advice is not to drink any alcohol at all.

1.3 Roles and responsibilities of parenthood

1. Food, clothing, shelter, warmth and rest/sleep.

2. Parents must provide somewhere safe for children to live. The home in which a child grows up has a huge impact on their childhood. Children who do not grow up in adequate homes are disadvantaged in terms of their health, safety and well-being. For example, a child who lives in damp conditions may develop asthma and/or frequent chest infections. It is important to a child's well-being that they feel sufficiently settled, safe and secure in their home.

3. Sufficient rest and sleep is crucial to a child's well-being, learning, growth and development. Without it, they will not thrive. This makes rest/sleep extremely important.

4. Children need to be supported in learning how to experience and manage their feelings. Parents can guide children by being an appropriate role model. Parents will also want to give their child an understanding of their family's customs and values. Parents also need to plan opportunities for their child to socialise with their peers.

1.4 Recognise and evaluate methods of contraception, their efficiency and reliability

1. The choices are the male or female condom, or a diaphragm.

2. Hormonal methods of contraception for women that come in two forms: the combined pill and the progestogen-only pill.

3. A woman records the symptoms in her body (by taking her temperature and monitoring bodily secretions, for example) that indicate when she

is fertile and able to conceive – around eight days in each month. On other days, she will be able to have sex without conceiving. On fertile days, a condom can be used, or the couple can abstain. This method is up to 98 per cent effective if used correctly.

1.5 The structure and function of male and female reproductive systems

1 During menstruation, blood flows from the uterus and leaves the body via the vagina. A new egg then develops in one of the ovaries. About 14 days after the first day of menstruation, the egg is released from the ovary and travels along the fallopian tube to the uterus. The lining of the uterus will be thickened and ready should the egg be fertilised by sperm. If this occurs, the baby will start to grow.

2 The sperm duct system consists of the epididymis, which contains the sperm, and the vas deferens, which are the sperm ducts (tubes) that sperm pass through. Glands produce semen, which mixes with the sperm and carries it. Conception/fertilisation occurs when a sperm penetrates an egg following ejaculation of sperm from the penis into the vagina.

3 Identical twins are conceived as the result of one fertilised egg dividing into two cells, causing two identical babies to grow in the uterus.

4 Non-identical twins are the result of two separate eggs being released and fertilised by two different sperm, causing two non-identical babies to grow in the uterus.

5 Missed period, breast changes, passing urine frequently, tiredness, nausea.

2.1 The roles of the different health professionals supporting the pregnant mother

1 Hospital midwives, community midwives, independent midwives.

2 A gynaecologist's role includes the care of mothers with complicated medical problems, emergency care for problems in early pregnancy, e.g. bleeding, and termination of a pregnancy, including pre-assessment and counselling.

3 A paediatrician is a doctor specialising in babies and children, whose role may include being present at the birth if there is a concern about a baby's health. If there is an unexpected concern

following the birth, a paediatrician is likely to be called. They may check a healthy baby over before it leaves hospital.

2.2 The importance of antenatal and parenting classes

1 Antenatal classes help with preparation for a safe pregnancy, labour and parenthood.

2 The father/partner can support the mother throughout pregnancy by providing practical support with tasks if she is feeling tired and being emotionally supportive if she is anxious about coping with birth. They can help the mother during labour and birth by massaging her back, shoulders or legs, supporting her body, timing contractions, giving encouragement, drinks, snacks or ice cubes, sponging her down, talking/finding ways to pass the time, helping her to find a comfortable position, making sure health professionals are aware of the birthing plan, learning relaxation and breathing techniques alongside the mother and participating alongside her during labour and birth.

3 Diet and exercise, the negative impact of smoking, alcohol and recreational drugs during pregnancy and after the birth, and the benefits of breastfeeding.

2.3 Routine checks carried out at an antenatal clinic, including scans

1 It is important to check for STIs because they can be harmful for an unborn baby. They can be more serious when caught during pregnancy, and can even be life-threatening for the mother and/or baby, so it is important to identify and treat them. STIs including chlamydia and gonorrhoea can be treated and cured with antibiotics. STIs caused by viruses, such as genital herpes, hepatitis B and HIV cannot be cured. These conditions may be treated to reduce the risk of them being passed to the baby.

2 An ultrasound dating scan checks how far along the pregnancy is, the baby's development, whether more than one baby is expected and that the baby is growing in the right place. Some abnormalities may be detected.

3 An examination of the uterus is performed to check how soft the cervix is; whether there is any thinning or opening of the cervix; the position of the cervix; how far into the pelvis the baby has descended; which way the baby is facing.

2.4 Specialised diagnostic tests

1 An ultrasound scan is a specialised diagnostic test carried out in weeks 18–21 of pregnancy. It checks for major physical abnormalities in the baby, but cannot find everything that might be wrong.

2 Two from:
   - Nuchal translucency (NT) test: indicates the likelihood of a baby having Down's syndrome.
   - Alpha fetoprotein (AFP) test: reveals whether a baby might have a condition such as spina bifida or anencephaly.
   - Chorionic villus sampling (CVS): checks for genetic disorders, e.g. Down's syndrome
   - An ultrasound scan: checks for major physical abnormalities in the baby.
   - Amniocentesis: tests for genetic disorders.

3 A CVS test carries a risk of miscarriage and infection, so not all mothers offered the test decide to go ahead. There is no cure for the majority of conditions detected.

2.5 The choices available for delivery

1 Hospital birth, home birth, Domino scheme, private hospital/independent midwife.

2 Parents who can afford it may decide to pay because they feel that the standard of the provision is higher. A private hospital is also a popular choice for families in the public eye.

3 Advantages of hospital births include: highly trained staff and equipment available in emergencies, which could save a baby's life and is reassuring; some pain relief can only be given in hospital; forceps, ventouse and caesarean section deliveries can only be carried out in hospital; midwives are on hand after the birth to help with issues such as feeding and can let a mother rest by taking a baby into the nursery; and the demands of home life are left behind.

2.6 The stages of labour and the methods of delivery, including pain relief

1 Stage one is the start of labour, in which the neck of the uterus opens and the uterus muscles start to contract and release. The bag of amniotic fluid around the baby bursts (the waters break). Stage two, the birth of the baby, starts when the cervix becomes fully dilated at 10 cm, and ends when the baby has been born. Stage 3 is the delivery of placenta and membranes, which follows straight after the birth of the baby.

2 Two from:
   - Forceps: a curved metal instrument that fits around the baby's head. They are carefully positioned, then joined together at the handles. As the mother pushes with a contraction, an obstetrician gently pulls to help deliver the baby. Some forceps are designed to turn the baby to the right position to be born.
   - Ventouse (vacuum extractor): a plastic or metal cup that fits firmly on the baby's head and is attached by suction. As the mother pushes with a contraction, an obstetrician gently pulls to help deliver the baby.
   - Caesarean section: an operation to deliver a baby through a cut made in the abdomen and womb. May be recommended as an elective (planned) procedure, or done in an emergency if a vaginal birth becomes unsafe. Reasons for a caesarean include: the baby being in the breech position (feet first); a low-lying placenta (placenta praevia); pre-eclampsia; infections such as STIs and untreated HIV; the baby not getting enough oxygen and nutrients, so needing to be delivered immediately; labour is not progressing; excessive vaginal bleeding.

3 Three from:
   - Gas and air (entonox): this mixture of oxygen and nitrous oxide gas does not remove all pain, but helps to reduce it.
   - Pethidine: quickly makes the mother feel relaxed because it causes the muscles to relax. This makes pain more tolerable, but it does not take it away altogether.
   - Epidural anaesthetic: local anaesthetic that numbs the nerves that carry the pain impulses from the birth canal to the brain. Can provide total pain relief, but is not always 100 per cent effective.
   - TENS: small electrical impulses are delivered, which give a tingling sensation. They reduce the pain signals going to the spinal cord and brain, relieving pain and relaxing muscles.
   - Water birth: water can help relaxation, and this makes contractions more bearable. The water should be kept at a comfortable temperature, not above 37.5°C.
   - Breathing and relaxation techniques: these can help a mother to relax and rest between contractions, and to cope with the pain when they occur.

3.1 The postnatal checks of the newborn baby

1 Five from:
  - Weight: tracked on centile charts, which show the expected pattern of growth of a healthy baby, so that comparisons can be made.
  - Length: recorded on centile charts, so growth can be tracked.
  - Head circumference: the shape of the head is assessed and the circumference measured and used to track development over the coming weeks/months.
  - Fontanelle: soft spots between the bones in the skull, where the skull bones have not yet fused together (the bones won't join together for a year or more).
  - Eyes: checked for cataracts and other conditions, through assessment of the appearance and movement of the eyes.
  - Mouth: a finger is placed in the mouth to check that the palate (roof of the mouth) is complete. The sucking reflex is also checked.
  - Feet: toes are counted and checked for webbing, the natural resting position of the feet and ankles are observed to check for talipes (clubfoot).
  - Hands: fingers are counted and checked for webbing. Palms are checked to see if two creases (palmar creases) run across them.
  - Hips: checked for 'developmental dysplasia of the hip', a condition in which the hip joints have not formed properly.
  - Reflexes: newborns are observed to see if they display the expected reflexes; if these do not occur naturally, the baby's body may be stimulated to elicit the reflex medics wish to see.

2 **Salmon patches (stork marks):** flat red/pink patches on eyelids, neck or forehead at birth. **Mongolian spots:** bluish patches of darker pigment, appearing mostly over the bottom and on black skin. These can be mistaken for bruises, but are harmless. **Infantile haemangiomas (strawberry marks):** raised marks, usually red, appearing anywhere on the body. These grow in the first six months but then shrink and disappear.

3 **Sucking reflex:** gently touch the roof of a baby's mouth and they will make sucking motions. This motion allows them to feed. **Rooting reflex:** when a baby's lips or cheek is touched, they move their head, searching for their mother's nipple/bottle teat to feed. **Grasp reflex:** if you touch a baby's palm, they will grasp your fingers with their fingers. **Standing and walking reflex:** when held upright with feet on a firm surface, newborns make stepping movements with their legs (but cannot take their weight). **Startle reflex:** if a baby wakes suddenly/hears a loud noise, they will make a fist with their hands and move stiff arms away from their body.

3.2 The specific needs of the pre-term (premature) baby

1 A baby born before week 37 of pregnancy is considered to be pre-term.

2 Pre-term babies are likely to have a weak immune system, making infection more likely, because they will not have been in the womb for sufficient time to develop and grow fully before birth. Babies born before 37 weeks are not developed enough to survive outside the womb without medical help.

3 One of:
  - If a gap in the roof of the mouth is picked up during the mouth check, the baby has a 'cleft palate'. This makes feeding difficult, and surgery is necessary.
  - If a baby has 'tongue-tie', the tongue is anchored to the bottom of the mouth by a piece of skin that is too short and tight. A simple procedure generally overcomes this immediately.

3.3 The postnatal provision available for the mother and baby and the postnatal needs of the family

1 Health visitors give families support from pregnancy until children are five. They ensure children are healthy and developing normally. When a child is ill, the GP is usually the first point of contact. GPs liaise with others, including health visitors. This is to ensure that families get necessary treatment, information and advice. A 6–8 week review will be carried out by a health visitor or doctor.

2 Taking time to bond with the new baby alongside the mother; helping and supporting the mother through difficult early days/weeks of motherhood; supporting the mother to take the time to take care of herself too, to stay fit and healthy, and to recover from the birth.

3 Support from family and close friends can be a huge help to new parents, especially if their relationship comes under pressure as they adjust to new responsibilities. Practical help and advice is valuable, e.g. helping with shopping, sharing childcare tips. Some new parents need a lot of support from those more experienced in childcare.

3.4 Conditions for development

1 **Love and security:** all children need to feel loved, wanted and nurtured, and kept physically secure and safe from harm. **Warmth:** children need warmth in order to be healthy and comfortable. **Rest/sleep:** vital to children's development and well-being. **Exercise/fresh air:** good for a child's physical health and well-being. Sufficient exercise builds fitness, robustness and helps strong growth and development. **Cleanliness:** children need clean and appropriately hygienic environments; the child must also be bathed daily and kept clean and fresh. Their clothing and bedding should be regularly laundered. **Stimulation/opportunities to play:** all children need opportunities to play in ways that are appropriate to their stage of development. **Opportunities for listening and talking:** these show a child that you care about them and are interested in them, and it is important to their social and emotional development, and intellectual and language development. **Routine** (including bedtime, bathtime, feeding): routines help young children to feel safe and secure; they also help adults to ensure that all of the child's care needs can be met effectively every day. **Awareness of Sudden Infant Death Syndrome (SIDS):** parents and carers should know how to take measures to prevent SIDS.

2 Parents and carers should know and follow this advice:
  – Always place your baby on their back to sleep.
  – Place your baby in the 'feet to foot' position (with their feet touching the end of the cot, Moses basket, or pram).
  – Keep your baby's head uncovered. Their blanket should be tucked in no higher than their shoulders.
  – Let your baby sleep in a cot or Moses basket in the same room as you for the first six months.
  – Use a mattress that is firm, flat, waterproof and in good condition.
  – Breastfeed your baby (if you can).
  – **Do not** smoke during pregnancy or let anyone smoke in the same room as your baby (both before and after birth).
  – **Do not** sleep on a bed, sofa or armchair with your baby.
  – **Do not** share a bed with your baby if you or your partner smoke or take drugs, or if you have been drinking alcohol.
  – **Do not** let your baby get too hot or too cold. A room temperature of 16–20°C, with light bedding or a lightweight baby sleeping bag, will provide a comfortable sleeping environment for your baby.

3 Promoting positive behaviour is by far the best way to limit inappropriate behaviour. When adults notice and praise specific positive behaviour, a child tends to feel proud of themselves, and they enjoy the approval they receive. This encourages them to repeat the socially acceptable behaviour, until it becomes an ingrained, normal part of what they do.

4.1 How immunity to disease and infection can be acquired

1 During pregnancy, antibodies from the mother are passed to the unborn baby through the placenta. Some immunity can also be passed on through breastfeeding.

2 Once a child has been vaccinated against a disease, their body can fight it off more successfully. If a child is not vaccinated, they are at higher risk of catching and becoming very ill from the illness. The NHS offers vaccines at 8 weeks, 12 weeks, 16 weeks, 1 year, 2–6 years old and 3 years 4 months. This is known as the 'routine immunisation schedule'. Vaccines protect against many diseases including diphtheria, tetanus, polio, measles, mumps, rubella and meningitis B and C.

3 There will always be some children who are unavoidably unprotected because they can't be vaccinated for medical reasons, they are too young to be vaccinated, they can't get to the vaccine clinics or the vaccine doesn't work (although this is rare).

4.2 How to recognise and treat common childhood ailments and diseases

1 Five from: vomiting and diarrhoea; high temperature; tiredness/disturbed sleep; reduced appetite; flushed or pale complexion/lip area; irritable/fretful behaviour; lack of desire to play; headache; swollen glands; runny/blocked up nose; cough.

2 The most common signs and symptoms of the common cold are a sore throat, sneezing, running nose, headache, slight fever, irritability and partial deafness.

3 Children with tonsillitis need plenty of rest and fluids. They need medical aid (to see a doctor) as antibiotics may be required. Iced drinks can help to relieve the pain.

4.3 When to seek treatment and help – the key signs and symptoms

1 The following signs and symptoms of illness indicate that you need to call for urgent medical attention (meaning you should call an ambulance): breathing difficulties; convulsions/seizures/fitting; child seems to be in significant pain; child is unresponsive – cannot easily or fully be roused from sleep, or a state of drowsiness; baby becomes unresponsive and/or their body seems to be floppy or limp; severe headache which may be accompanied by a stiff neck or a dislike of light; rash that remains (does not fade) when pressed with a glass; vomiting that persists for over 24 hours; unusual, high-pitched crying in babies; high fever/temperature that cannot be lowered; will not drink fluids – this is most worrying in babies.

2 You should take steps to lower a temperature by ensuring that warm clothing is removed so that just a cool layer is worn, and providing a cool drink, either water or another drink diluted with water. Some children may be given paracetamol syrup by parents or carers.

3 A doctor must be called immediately, because meningitis can be life-threatening, and the child might deteriorate quickly. If they cannot be contacted or are delayed, call 999 (or 112 from a mobile) for an ambulance. Do not wait for all of the symptoms to appear. If a casualty has already seen a doctor but is becoming worse, seek urgent medical attention again – call for an ambulance. Reassure the casualty and keep them cool until help arrives.

4 When an asthma attack occurs, the airways go into spasm, making breathing difficult. This may occur after contact with allergens such as dust, pollen or pet hair. It can also be caused by the child having a cold, experiencing stress or extreme cold. The casualty may cough, wheeze and become breathless. If a child is known to be asthmatic, they should have a 'reliever' inhaler immediately available. Reassure them and give the inhaler as instructed. Sit the casualty upright and leaning forwards in a comfortable position – they should never lie down. Stay with them. If this is the first attack or the condition persists or worsens, call for an ambulance.

4.4 Diet-related illnesses

1 It is very important to ensure that you fully understand children's dietary requirements so that you can meet their needs without error. In a setting, practitioners should ensure that full details of diet restrictions are recorded on a child's registration form. They must also communicate the child's requirements to everyone involved in caring for them. A list of the child's requirements should be displayed in the kitchen and eating area to remind all staff. You must never give a child food or drink without checking that it is safe for them to have. This also applies to raw cooking ingredients or food used in play that is not intended for consumption. Some children may need to eat at certain times of the day, and they might take medication daily. Children may have medication to take if they show symptoms of their condition or if you become aware that they have eaten – or in the case of some children, even touched – a food they should not have. You must ensure that you are absolutely clear about what to do for an individual child, and you must know how to recognise their symptoms.

2 Six from: red, itchy rash or blotchy skin that becomes raised; swelling of face, hands, feet; pale or flushed skin; puffy/red/itchy/watery eyes; wheezing/difficulty breathing; swelling of tongue and throat; abdominal pain; vomiting/diarrhoea; agitation/confusion; signs of shock.

3 You can help children achieve a healthy weight by encouraging 60 minutes of physically active play each day; providing healthy meals, drinks and snacks; keeping to child-size portions; ensuring children get sufficient sleep; being a good role model (e.g. eating healthily and being physically active).

4 Signs and symptoms of a hypoglycaemic attack (hypo) include drowsiness with a deteriorating level of response; feeling weak or faint; feeling hungry; confusion or irritability/behaving irrationally; palpitations; muscle tremors (trembling); sweating and cold, clammy, pale skin; rapid pulse.

4.5 The needs of an ill child

1 Usual routines often need to be adjusted to allow for extra naps, particularly if night-time sleep has been disturbed (for example by coughing or vomiting). Children's diets may need to be adjusted (if they have an upset stomach for example).

2 Two from: clinging to an adult's legs; sucking their thumb; wanting a dummy; wanting to be fed; wanting to sleep in a parent or carer's room, etc.

3 Three from: stories; colouring; puzzles; IT devices, etc.

4.6 How to prepare a child for a stay in hospital

1 Three from:
- It is very helpful to take children for a hospital/ward visit, as children are often afraid of the unknown. Seeing where they will sleep, meeting staff, etc., can help them to feel less worried.
- Acting out fears through hospital games can also help.
- There are many books and DVDs that help make the hospital world more familiar too.
- You should always explain what will happen in hospital, with honesty.

2 This helps a child to prepare for real-life situations, and gives them reassurance.

3 Parents can often continue with many aspects of the child's care, such as feeding, bathing and changing nappies. In some circumstances, they may even be able to sleep on the ward or in the building.

5.1 How to create a safe, child-friendly environment

1 A practitioner thinks carefully about a particular space, and identifies all of the apparent hazards. They then take steps to reduce the risk of the hazard causing harm to an acceptable level.

2 Ensure that children do not have access to chemicals unsafe for children to handle, sharp equipment, hot taps and hot water; prevent unsupervised access to water (drowning risk); prevent access to items unhygienic for children to handle (toilet brush, etc.), or items that are slippery when wet; prevent access to a window from which a child could fall.

3 First find the safest place to cross. Stop just before you get to the kerb. Look all around for traffic and listen. If traffic is coming, let it pass. When it is safe, go straight across the road – do not run. Keep looking and listening for traffic while you cross.

5.2 Safety labelling

1 **BSI safety mark/kitemark:** a UK product and service quality certification mark, administered by the British Standards Institution (BSI). **Lion Mark:** appears on toys that have been made by a member of the British Toy and Hobby Association and Toy Fair. **Age advice symbol:** identifies when equipment or a product isn't suitable for children under the age of 36 months (in the opinion of the manufacturer). **CE symbol:** the most common toy label and the first one to look for.

2 The CE symbol is the most common toy label and the first one to look for because by law, it has to be displayed on all new toys on the market in the EU. The CE logo proves that the toy has been tested for compliance with EU standards. It is also the manufacturer's declaration that the item meets all toy safety requirements.

3 You should look for a label confirming that all children's night garments (including dressing gowns) meet the flammability performance requirements. This includes garments for babies. Stretch garments such as baby-grows should be treated as children's nightwear.

5.3 Be aware of the most common childhood accidents

1 Stop the flow of electricity before approaching, or you are likely to receive an electric shock. Turn off power at the mains/master switch. If that is not possible, the child may be pushed or pulled well away from the source using a material that will not conduct the electricity. A first aider will learn how to do this safely on a first aid course (e.g. looping a thick towel around the feet to enable a child to be pulled from the source, or using a wooden broom to push them away). Once safe, approach the child. If the heart has stopped, an ambulance is needed. Check the airway, breathing and circulation and start CPR. Electricity can cause burns at the entry and exit points, which must be treated with cold water. Water and electricity are a very dangerous combination, so be sure the electricity source is off/the child is far enough away from it. Urgent or emergency medical attention will be needed, depending on the burns.

2 Drowning occurs in natural water bodies such as the sea and rivers, and also in man-made places, such as pools, canals, lakes, ponds and baths.

Babies and young children can drown in as little as 2.5 cm of water.

3 An infant or young child with any burn needs to go to hospital straight away.
   - Cool the area with water for at least ten minutes, preferably by holding it under gently running tap water.
   - Remove any jewellery, watches, belts or restrictive clothing that isn't stuck to the burn/scald before swelling occurs.
   - Cover the burn/scald with clean cling film or place a clean plastic bag over a foot or hand. Cling film should be applied lengthways, instead of being wrapped around a limb, due to the risk of swelling. If cling film/bags are not available, a sterile dressing may be used.

5.4 Social safety

1 Explain to the child what a stranger is, and what to do if they are approached. If an unknown person talks to them, they don't need to worry about being rude – they can walk away quickly, telling an adult if they feel worried. If a stranger asks or tells a child to go with them, the child should run away and tell a safe adult immediately. They must learn to 'Say no, never go!' If children are touched, grabbed or feel frightened or worried that they are in danger, it is alright to break the usual behaviour rules: they should attract attention by shouting and screaming, and punch and kick, if they feel they need to.

2 Use child-friendly search engines, or alternatively, turn on the safe search settings on the traditional search engines. Children should also be told not to: give out personal information; supply registration details without asking for permission and help; visit chat websites or social networking sites without asking for permission and help; arrange to meet an online friend in person without parental knowledge and permission (if a parent agrees to let them, they should always go along with them); give any indication of their age or sex in a personal email address or screen name; keep anything that worries or upsets them online secret from you; respond to unwanted emails or other messages.

3 Children should stop and look all around for the adult they are with. If they can't see them, they should approach a safe person – a police officer, CPO, crossing point patrol guard (lollipop person), cashier at a till in a shop or lastly a parent with children. They should wait outside until their adult, parent or a police officer comes to look after them. They should not go anywhere with strangers.